D0146925

THE COLLECTED WORKS OF
ERIC VOEGELIN

VOLUME 27

THE NATURE OF
THE LAW
AND RELATED
LEGAL WRITINGS

PROJECTED VOLUMES IN THE SERIES

THE COLLECTED WORKS OF

ERIC VOEGELIN

VOLUME 27

THE NATURE OF
THE LAW
AND RELATED
LEGAL WRITINGS

EDITED BY

ROBERT ANTHONY PASCAL,
JAMES LEE BABIN,
AND
JOHN WILLIAM CORRINGTON

LOUISIANA STATE UNIVERSITY PRESS

BATON ROUGE AND LONDON

00 99 98 97 96 95 94 93 92 91   1 2 3 4 5

Typeface: Trump Mediaevel
Typesetter: G & S Typesetters, Inc.
Printer and binder: Thomson-Shore, Inc.

Library of Congress Cataloging-in-Publication Data

Voegelin, Eric, 1901–
    The nature of the law, and related legal writings / edited by Robert Anthony
Pascal, James Lee Babin, and John William Corrington.
    p.   cm. — (The Collected works of Eric Voegelin ; v. 27)
    Includes index.
    Contents: The nature of the law — Outline of jurisprudence course —
Supplementary notes for students in jurisprudence course — Right
and might — Two recent contributions to the science of law — The
theory of legal science.
    ISBN 0-8071-1673-4 (cloth)
    1. Jurisprudence. I. Pascal, Robert Anthony. II. Babin, James
Lee. III. Corrington, John William. IV. Title. V. Series:
Voegelin, Eric, 1901– Works. 1989 ; v. 27.
B3354.V88 1989 vol. 27
[K230.V63]
193 s—dc20
[340]   90-28744
                                                                                    CIP

The editors offer grateful acknowledgment to the
Earhart Foundation and to the Foundation for Faith
in Search of Understanding for support provided at various stages
in the preparation of this book for publication.

Contents

Editors' Preface

The editing of this volume was begun by John William Corrington, at one time of the English faculty at Louisiana State University and then of the English faculty at Loyola University in New Orleans, later a Louisiana attorney, television script writer, and, of special relevance here, a very ardent student of Eric Voegelin's thought. After his unanticipated death in November, 1988, the task was accepted by the present editors, Robert Anthony Pascal and James Lee Babin, respectively professor of law emeritus and assistant professor of English at Louisiana State University. The present editors are fortunate to have had available to them both the manuscript of *The Nature of the Law* as edited by Mr. Corrington and also his insightful notes on it and other writings in this volume made in anticipation of preparing an introduction to them.

The legal writings of Eric Voegelin contained in this volume are *The Nature of the Law* (1957), a copyrighted monograph never before edited for general publication but mimeographed for distribution to students in the course in jurisprudence at the Louisiana State University Law School; The "Outline of Jurisprudence Course" and "Supplementary Notes" distributed to jurisprudence students from 1954 through 1957, neither otherwise published; and reviews of four books on legal science and legal philosophy. These reviews, published in 1941 and 1942, are of James Brown Scott's *Law, the State, and the International Community* (1939); N. S. Timasheff's *An Introduction to the Sociology of Law* (1939); Edgar Bodenheimer's *Jurisprudence* (1940); and Huntington Cairns's *The Theory of Legal Science* (1941).

Not all of Eric Voegelin's works with legal content have been included in this volume. Those predominantly on political science or political philosophy have been excluded here but may appear in other volumes of *The Collected Works of Eric Voegelin*. There are, however, two distinctly legal works that have not been included in this volume: his 1927 article "Kelsen's Pure Theory of Law" and the chapter (in translation) "Anglo-American Analytic Jurisprudence" from his *Ueber die Form des amerikanischen Geistes* (1928), to be published in English as Volume 1 of the *Collected Works* under the title *On The Form of the American Mind*. Both deal with analytical jurisprudence, a dominant interest of Voegelin during his student years under Hans Kelsen and later while he was seeking appointment as *Privat Dozent* in law at the University of Vienna. The editors considered these two works too narrow in scope to be included in the same volume with *The Nature of the Law* and the jurisprudence course "Outline" and "Supplementary Notes."

Something must be said of the principles adhered to by the editors. The several book reviews have been reprinted as published except for the correction of printers' misspellings and changes in punctuation, prepositions, and pronouns more consistent with current style. Two versions of the "Outline of Jurisprudence Course" were discovered. One does not have what appears in the second and presumably revised version as the topic "I. Delimitation of the Field." Thus the second and more complete version has been reproduced in this volume. No changes were made in it except to add in brackets two phrases intended as clarifications. The texts of the various "Supplementary Notes" distributed to jurisprudence students in mimeographed form have been reproduced unchanged except in punctuation, capitalization, the italicization of book titles and foreign words, the re-enumeration of outline sections and subsections for consistency, and rare changes of word order, verb tenses, prepositions, and pronouns to conform to better usage.

In the judgment of the present editors, *The Nature of the Law* required some editing. Mr. Corrington had edited most minimally, restricting himself to an occasional punctuation or word change and to the infrequent division of very long sentences or paragraphs into two or more. The present editors, treating the mimeographed monograph for what it was, a manuscript that had not undergone editing by someone other than the author, believed it required more than Mr. Corrington had dared give it. At the same time, recognizing that Voegelin himself could not be shown the edited manuscript, the editors have done nothing that in their judgment might result in the least modification of the author's meaning. Punctuation has been made to conform more to present American usage, care being taken, nevertheless, to preserve or to introduce not strictly necessary punctuation where it might assist the reader. More divisions of sentences and paragraphs were introduced. The language being on the whole in the personal active present discursive mode, sentences in passive voice and impersonal style were made to accord. The order of words, phrases, and clauses often was changed for the sake of clarity. Often prepositions required changing and infrequently a preferable synonym was substituted. Only rarely was it necessary to insert a clarifying word or phrase. Additions by the editors to the manuscript proper were placed in brackets. Page references were added to the table of contents of *The Nature of the Law*. The Index was prepared by the editors.

The editors wish to acknowledge the generosity of the Paul M. Hebert Law Center of Louisiana State University in providing secretarial and material assistance for this project. They also wish to thank Mrs. Sandra Saale for her willing, efficient, and cheerful typing of the manuscript and for making the computer search in preparation for the indexing.

Editors' Introduction

The Nature of the Law was written while Voegelin was teaching jurisprudence in the Law School of Louisiana State University and appeared in 1957 in a mimeographed "temporary edition exclusively for the use of students registered in" that course. Voegelin never revised the monograph, even though he once informed one of the editors of the present volume that he was contemplating doing so and in 1976 entered into correspondence with the Notre Dame University Press with a view toward its publication. Nor does it appear that the monograph ever was distributed to the students in jurisprudence. Voegelin had taught the course in the spring semesters of 1954 through 1957 and probably had completed the last offering before the monograph had been mimeographed. Then in January, 1958, he left Louisiana State University to accept professorships in political science and history and the direction of the Institute of Political Science at the University of Munich.

The Nature of the Law is Voegelin's only comprehensive and systematic text on law. It is a product of the mature Voegelin. He wrote it at a time when he had settled upon the necessity of abandoning his original plan of writing a history of political ideas, published *The New Science of Politics* and the first three volumes of *Order and History*, and taught the course in jurisprudence four years.[1] He had come to realize that ideas do not have a history, that only people do, and that their history consists of their successes

1. Eric Voegelin, *Autobiographical Reflections* (Baton Rouge, 1989), 62–64; Voegelin, *The New Science of Politics: An Introduction* (Chicago, 1952); the first three volumes of Voegelin's *Order and History* are: *Israel and Revelation*, Vol. I, *The World of the Polis*, Vol. II, and *Plato and Aristotle*, Vol. III (Baton Rouge, 1956, 1957).

and failures in the differentiation of their noetic and pneumatic experiences of life under God. For the same reason, he had come to realize that law cannot have a history apart from the history of the society whose order it articulates, and that its essence, or nature, is precisely the structure of the society whose law it is.

Voegelin had come to these understandings through his own reflections, prompted, as he would have said, by the opposition in his soul to his experiences of phenomena in the external world indicating disorder. Thus at age twenty-three he expressed dissatisfaction with Hans Kelsen's limitation of the concept "State" to that of "pure law," that is, law divorced from ontological criteria of order and reduced to a scheme of governmental responses to existential conditions and actions internally consistent with a posited basic norm. Another and more serious instance, to simplify a complex set of experiences, was his reaction to German national socialism, fascism, and Marxist-Leninist communism.[2] These experiences led him to search for the sources of true criteria for human order by which the phenomena of society and law might be judged.

Voegelin's studies led him to discover that philosophy properly so called is man's symbolic articulation and differentiation of his noetic (rational) experiences of being, insights into reality and its implications made possible by his participation in the "In-Between" of matter and spirit, and not, as had come to pass since Enlightenment days, an attempt to mold reality into a scheme consistent with a posited or assumed idea (ideology); and they led him to conclude that revelation is man's differentiation and symbolization of pneumatic, or spiritual, experiences offered him through divine grace. Voegelin realized, too, that even though men could accept on faith the symbolic representation of the noetic and pneumatic experiences of those who had had them, knowledge of these experiences could be attained only by reconstructing the experiences that had led to the symbolizations.[3]

It was in this spirit that Voegelin presented the Walgreen Lectures at the University of Chicago in 1951 (published as *The New*

2. Eric Voegelin, "Reine Rechtslehre und Staatslehre," *Zeitschrift fuer Oeffentliches Recht*, IV (1924), 80–131; Voegelin, *Autobiographical Reflections*, 24, 25, 45–53.

3. For a full account of Voegelin's intellectual journey, see Ellis Sandoz, *The Voegelinian Revolution* (Baton Rouge, 1981).

Science of Politics in 1952) and later composed the first three volumes of *Order and History* (1956–1957); and it is in the same spirit that he wrote *The Nature of the Law*.

In *The Nature of the Law*, Voegelin forces the reader to analyze the everyday phenomena of law to discover its nature, or essence, and its attributes, beginning with the words used in ordinary discourse about the law, rejecting putative insights and assumptions that prove fallacious by being found inconsistent with this or that experience with the law, and retaining those that accord with them and advance our understanding, until at last the law is understood to have as its ontological nature the structure of the society whose law it is and to have as its criterion man's relation to being as we can know it through philosophy and revelation. Thus *The Nature of the Law* is a modern instance of philosophizing in the classical style.

From beginning to end, Voegelin is relentless in the analysis for essence. He begins with the observation that though we speak of "the law" as if it were singular, actually it exists in a plurality of orders whose contents are not identical. "The law," however, cannot be a "species" individuated in many orders, for all legal rules are "essential" in their respective legal orders. Nor can "the law" be a single example of a "species" including all rules of all legal orders, for essence then would be reduced to a catalog of all legal rules in all orders, and that would be nonsense. The essence of the law proving elusive for the moment, Voegelin directs his attention to the "validity" of the law. Laws, he observes, come into validity and cease to be valid, raising the question whether "the law" is a series of momentarily valid aggregates of rules or a changing entity given unity by a process. These constructions prove to be unsatisfactory as well, and so, guided by these preliminary results, Voegelin shifts the analysis away from law as an isolated phenomenon and toward law in its social context.

In this context, Voegelin observes, "law" in its most fundamental descriptive meaning is the substance of order in any realm of being—the law of gravity, for example, in the realm of material being. The lawmaking process, then, is seen to be the means of securing the substance of order among human beings in society. From this perspective Voegelin lists the principal theoretical constructions of the relation of the lawmaking processes and the substance of order. For Plato and Aristotle, the philosophers ascertain the content of true order, and the law is formulated to secure it. With the advent of the national state, the prince articulates the positive law in conformity with divine and natural law, with natural law alone, or simply according to his discretion. With secularism and the disintegration of philosophy, the question of the substance of true order is ignored and all emphasis is placed on the positive lawmaking process. Finally, in sociological jurisprudence the only effort is to describe legal phenomena without advancing to an analysis of the law's nature. It becomes clear, nevertheless, that it is in the order of society that the law's nature must be sought, and Voegelin proceeds in Chapter III to analyze "The Complex of Order" in society.

In beginning the analysis of the complex of order, Voegelin notes the tensions between true substantive order and the lawmaking process, on the one hand, and between true substantive order and the social order as it exists, on the other. Regarding the first tension, Voegelin notes that the "weight" of the relation is toward the social side of the complex, and he illustrates this fact with the observation that the validity of changes in constitutional structure cannot be explained in terms of a procedural process, but only in terms of a continuous society whose order is shaped by reference to extralegal sources. These extralegal sources, he observes, include the authority of the power structure in the society articulating an order that is intended to conform to the ontologically true criteria for substantive human order under the existential conditions. "The law" thus involves more than legal rules; it encompasses all the efforts of human beings to establish order in a concrete society.

Voegelin then examines the second type of tensions, between existing social orders and true substantive order. Social order, he observes, has the quality of lastingness, so much so that the legal order, to the extent it is obeyed, can be said to describe an existing society, much in the way "the laws of nature" describe determined existential phenomena. It is not the function of legal rules, however, to describe the order of society, for the order of society, unlike that of determined existential phenomena, is not inherent in it. Rather, it must be supplied by human action in the form of legal rules, and thus the rules come to be seen as normative. Yet the rules are to be discovered rather than made, and there is always tension between true order and the realized existential order. This tension exists because man has the experience of participating in an order of being that includes not only man, but also God, the world, and society; because he experiences the need to be attuned to the order of being; and because he also experiences that his attunement to the order of being is dependent on his action. This tension is the ontological source of the Ought, or normativity, of legal rules.

Because the rule is normative, it must be communicated to the people, and this communication, ultimately, is through the services of the legal profession. Voegelin here elaborates in order to differentiate legal rules in effect and projects for law. Among the latter are projects proposed for adoption or enactment, projects intended to serve as models for imitation under existential circumstances, and projects of philosophers intended to articulate true order, whether or not they can be enacted in the present or the future. In this last instance, the true order is experienced as such in the soul of the philosopher, order oriented toward the full unfolding of his nature. In the empirical lawmaking process, the source of normativity is the effort to participate in true order thus discovered.

In the context of the tensions between the lawmaking process and the social order, on one side, and true substantive order, on the other, Voegelin stresses the self-organizing character of society and the impersonal character of legal rules, factors that render "command" theories of law inadequate. This self-organization of society inevitably is accomplished through representatives of society, however they may come to power. Although the order proclaimed by the representatives may not conform in particulars to a citizen's sense of good order, it must be obeyed by all as citizens, if the general social good is to be realized. Some error in translating the ontologically true order into existing order is unavoidable, for truth in matters of order, especially in particulars, rarely can be determined certainly. The judgment of the representatives of society must prevail, therefore, and force is necessary to assure compliance on the part of the recalcitrant.

In the conclusion, Voegelin summarizes the components of validity of legal rules: first, legal rules have ontological existence, not of themselves, but only in their social context; second, as legal rules are propositions about human behavior, their normativity must be determined in terms of their fitness to provide an order in which every person's potential can be realized; and, third, the fitness of legal rules for providing this order must be ascertained through philosophy and revelation. Further, the content of a legal order cannot be derived from the nature of man, for law always exists in a social context, and the organization of society, always concrete, must be such as to accomplish the end of society as well as possible under existential conditions. Finally, because law is only part of the social context, there is no history of law, but only history of societies; and in this history the most important events have been the differentiation of Reason and Revelation from Cosmological Myth.

The Nature of the Law may be characterized as a reasoned invitation to restore holiness to the legal order. As the nature of the law emerges with increasing clarity from Voegelin's analysis, none of the historically recent and dominant conceptions of the law prove adequate. "The law" is not simply a "command" of a Leviathan to persons who, out of fear of a worse situation, have surrendered all right to object. It is not simply the result of a social compact among autonomous individuals by which they surrender to each other aspects of an unlimited license in the effort to avoid harm from each other. It is not just the expressed will of a majority securing its own self-defined, immediate worldly interest, or that of a dominant class seeking the eventual attainment of a falsely conceived worldly millennium. The analysis, rather, shows the law to be part of the order a society generates for itself, through its representatives, in the effort to attain the common good. Accordingly, a specific legal order may be judged by the degree to which it secures for each and every person, a being spiritual as well as material, now living or to come, the possibility of developing to the fullest one's capacity to participate in the life that by creation each shares with God and other persons. The law and its institutions specify the modes of cooperation judged proper and advantageous under present circumstances to achieve that common good. The measure of the law, in last analysis, is social order consistent with the fullness of reality.

The "Outline of Jurisprudence Course" (1954–1957) is concerned more with the criteria for legal order discovered through philosophy and revelation than it is with the law's essence or nature, which was the primary subject of *The Nature of the Law*. The two, therefore, are complementary. Although *The Nature of the Law* did not appear in mimeographed form until Voegelin had given the course for the last time, Voegelin lectured on this subject, as well as on the criteria for law, in the jurisprudence course. Indeed, it may be hazarded that had Voegelin taught the course again after preparing *The Nature of the Law* in mimeographed form, he would have made the monograph the basis of the first part of the course and revised the outline accordingly.

Consistent with Voegelin's conclusion in *The Nature of the Law*—that the law cannot have an ontological existence separate from that of the society whose structure of order it is—the "Outline" considers the criteria for law from the view of the criteria for social order as unfolded historically. Thus the "Outline" reflects the development already given in 1952 in *The New Science of Politics* and later more elaborately in *Order and History*. Some of these matters are taken up as well in *The Nature of the Law*, but only insofar as necessary to discover through analysis the nature, or essence, of the law. The lectures in the jurisprudence course, of which there seem to be no written versions, were more complete on that subject. The jurisprudence course, however, as the "Outline" attests, was not presented in a historically linear fashion. Facing students who often had little or no background for his lectures, he first "delimited the field" by providing a framework of understanding. Then he proceeded to discuss Justinian's legislatively defined definition of jurisprudence and its component elements. Next he presented the primary experiences of social order—the cosmic order in China, Babylon, and Egypt; the revealed will of God in Israel; participation of the psyche in the divine logos in Hellenic Greece; and participation in the spirit of Christ in Christianity. These considerations led to discussions of the legal cultures in the Near East and the West, and then to the manner in which social crises through history have prompted reflections on the meaning of law, from the case of Israel and the Prophets to that of the high Middle Ages and Saint Thomas Aquinas. Next, Voegelin analyzed the gradual deterioration of adequate conceptions of law, beginning with the weakening and end of Christendom and the simultaneous rise of national states, the eventual surfacing of positive law when both revelation and philosophy came to be considered irrelevant to order, the emergence of history and immanentist thought as bases for law, and contemporary trends in legal philosophy. The last part of the course, finally, was an account of the return to primary experiences of order in the present century, an enterprise in which Voegelin himself was a major participant.

The "Supplementary Notes" for students in the jurisprudence course are in themselves a compact course in the subject. Voegelin considers, though not in this order, the necessity of truth in communication; the impossibility of a fully rational science of action (including law) unless there is a highest good to which all human actions can be ordered; the hierarchy of goods according to Aristotle; the experiences of transcendence (participation in transcendent being, revelation, grace, and a "mankind" of all who have lived, are living, or will live). Having laid this foundation, Voegelin proceeds to list nine "principles of Jurisprudence" by which the legal cultures of the three main types of civilization—the cosmological, the anthropological, and the soteriological—might be appraised: 1) the constancy of human nature; 2) the progress of self-understanding (with regard to man's position in the world and his relation to transcendent reality) from compactness to differentiation; 3) the growth of knowledge through the differentiation of experiences and their symbolization, and the degrees of rationality in various symbolizations; 4) the observation that all civilizations experience order located in transcendent reality, though with different degrees of differentiation; 5) the affinity (consubstantiality) of the experiencing soul for the transcendent reality; 6) the nature of cognition in experience of transcendence (participation) as a response to transcendent reality (e.g., Christian faith as the proof of things unseen); 7) the impossibility of defining just order because of its origin in transcendent reality and the impossibility of deducing a system of rules from highest axioms; 8) the rarity of the highest degrees of sensitive response to transcendent reality (as with Aristotle, the Israelite prophets, or Saint Paul) and the necessity of studying the classic sources in order to understand these experiences and thereby to attune the soul to reality; and 9) the progress of the understanding of just order through reaction of the soul to concrete injustice.

The final segment of the "Supplementary Notes," in a sense an appendix, is on "natural law," the various uses of the term, and appraisals of them.

Voegelin also distributed to his jurisprudence students a mimeographed manuscript entitled "The Symbolization of Order," copyrighted in 1954, to supplement his lectures. The manuscript was identical with the Introduction to Volume I of *Order and History*, published in 1956, and it is not reprinted here.

The legal ideas of the mature Voegelin, reflected in *The Nature of the Law* and in the jurisprudence course "Outline" and "Supplementary Notes," had developed only gradually, he tells us, during the years 1943 to 1950. His earliest publications of a distinctly legal character were of a much narrower scope. Thus the 1927 article "Kelsen's Pure Theory of Law" and the chapter (in translation) "Anglo-American Analytic Jurisprudence" in *Ueber die Form des amerikanischen Geistes* (1928) evidenced an interest in analytic jurisprudence that seems to have fascinated him during his student years under Hans Kelsen and even later, when, after his return from studies in the United States and France, he was seeking appointment as *Privat Dozent* in law at the University of Vienna.[4]

Yet it must not be assumed that Voegelin was ever a logical positivist. He seems to have insisted always that the sciences of human order take into full account man's position in reality. His dissertation in Vienna in 1922, for example (Voegelin tells us, for apparently a copy does not exist), was on "the ontological [problem] of constructing social reality out of relations between autonomous individuals or of assuming a preexistent spiritual bond between human beings." Then, in 1924, he criticized Kelsen for distorting reality by limiting the concept of state to "pure law" devoid of cultural and philosophical content. By 1928 or 1929, Voegelin says, he had come to realize that a political theory (and

---

4. Voegelin, *Autobiographical Reflections*, 62–64; Eric Voegelin, *Anamnesis*, trans. Gerhart Niemeyer (1978; rpr. Springfield, Mo., 1990), 9–13; Eric Voegelin, "Kelsen's Pure Theory of Law," *Political Science Quarterly*, XLII (1927), 268–76. Kelsen's *Allgemeine Staatslehre*, summarizing and augmenting his previous works based on his *pure theory of law*, had appeared in 1925 while Voegelin was studying in the United States; Eric Voegelin, *Ueber die Form des amerikanischen Geistes* (Tuebingen, 1928); Voegelin, *Autobiographical Reflections*, 38. On the publication of *Der Autoritaere Staat* (Vienna, 1936) he was advanced in rank to associate professor, teaching administrative law (Sandoz, *The Voegelinian Revolution*, 48).

therefore, we may conclude, a legal theory as well) "had to be based on classical and Christian philosophy." Between 1929 and 1942, of course, his experiences with German national socialism served to intensify his researches on the foundations of human order, and these confirmed his judgment that political (and legal) theory must be based on all of reality and not on some of it or on posited or false criteria.[5]

The years 1938 to 1942, which we may call his transitional years, were also his first in the United States as a permanent resident, the years in which he was attempting to secure his position in the American academic world.[6] Possibly he was not certain whether he would settle in a political science faculty or a law faculty. Either association would have suited Voegelin quite well, given the direction of his developing thought; but this possible uncertainty may explain why, in 1941 and 1942, he published reviews of four books on legal science and legal philosophy.

Each of the reviews makes its points. In that of James Brown Scott's *Law, the State, and the International Community* (1939), Voegelin chides the renowned author for asserting the thesis that law has been evolving toward the expression of good legal order, attempting to support it "by the authority of congenial thinkers" only, and ignoring much in the history of law that does not support his claims. Voegelin also criticizes the author for seemingly not recognizing that a power structure in society is as necessary for the introduction and maintenance of good order as it is capable of producing bad order.

The remaining reviews are of books on legal science or legal theory. Voegelin finds all of them deficient in that they do not bring together all factors relevant to a complete theory of law. His kindest thoughts are for Edgar Bodenheimer's *Jurisprudence* (1940), for at least the author seeks to present his subject in terms of the manner in which men, at various times in history, have experienced the phenomenon of law and sought to symbolize their experiences. Al-

---

5. Voegelin, *Autobiographical Reflections*, 26; Voegelin, "Reine Rechtslehre und Staatslehre." See also *Autobiographical Reflections*, 21, 22; *Autobiographical Reflections*, 38, 24, 25, 45–53.

6. Voegelin arrived in the United States in 1938, taught one semester at Harvard University, then at Bennington College and at the University of Alabama. In 1942, he joined the Government Department faculty at Louisiana State University and remained there until 1958 (Voegelin, *Autobiographical Reflections*, 57–59).

though Voegelin does not believe Bodenheimer has gone far enough in his analyses or discussions to produce a critical work of legal theory, he asserts that the work provides an excellent history of the theory of law and is appropriate for use as a text on the subject. N. S. Timasheff's *Sociology of Law* (1939), on the other hand, Voegelin regards as inadequate because the method of positivistic sociology cannot reach all the reality that bears upon the subject of law. He does not deny the immense learning of the author or the value of his work within its limited scope, but insists that abstractions from observable phenomena of a legal character cannot support an adequate theory of what law essentially is and should be.

It is in the review of Huntington Cairns's *The Theory of Legal Science* (1941) that Voegelin states most emphatically his insistence that a theory of law cannot be based on a natural science model and proceeds to detail what a theory of legal science must take into account. Measured by Voegelin's standards, Cairns's book was a failure. Cairns asserted that a *social* science of law—intending one modeled on the natural sciences—did not exist, but that one should be constructed, though it would take the efforts of many scholars over many years. The method for this construction, according to Cairns, would be, first, to collect data on human legal behavior, to observe its patterns, and to abstract from them general descriptive and predictive principles—more or less the procedure advocated by Timasheff. The second effort would be to create, through the analysis of the solutions reached in many particular problems over years, a body of empirically based ethical principles. These ethical principles, finally, could be employed, with the knowledge gained about human legal behavior, to develop general principles of a legal science directed toward the elimination of disorder and the creation of order.

Again, Voegelin's critique essentially was that a social science cannot be founded validly on the assumption that man is only matter, ignoring man's historical experience of his spirituality and all he had learned of himself. By ignoring all of history and assuming humanity can be treated simply as a *tabula rasa*, or as clay to be molded, Cairns was being only pseudoscientific. Voegelin's critique of Cairns, of course, is a critique of all would-be social science that ignores man's spirituality, and herein lies its principal merit.

Cairns's brief comments on Voegelin's critique were printed at the end of Voegelin's review.[7] One might be tempted to conclude that Cairns had not understood Voegelin's essential observation, that a science of law could not be based on empirical phenomena alone, for he insisted on the possibility of a legal science on a natural-science model and asserted that his book was "not historical." Cairns, however, also stated that he would not analyze "Voegelin's ontology." Thus it may be correct to say that Cairns understood Voegelin's comment, but that rejecting man's spirituality and the possibility of knowledge through philosophy and revelation, as the book attests amply, he could not hope for a legal science other than one modeled on natural science.

The reader who has read Cairns's book may be disappointed with Voegelin's review in one respect. Voegelin took Cairns to task at length and repeatedly for alleging that a legal science did not exist, though Cairns appears to have said only that a *social* science of law, meaning one modeled on the natural sciences alone, did not exist. Voegelin's remarks based on that possible misunderstanding of Cairns, however, do not detract from the substantive merit of his basic critique.

The four reviews mentioned above may be seen in retrospect as preparations for the organization of the jurisprudence course and the writing of *The Nature of the Law*, even though more than a decade separated them. Probably Voegelin would have proceeded to the latter more quickly had he become a member of a faculty of law rather than of political science.

ROBERT A. PASCAL
JAMES L. BABIN

7. See *Louisiana Law Review*, IV (1942), 571–72.

1

The Nature of the Law

THE NATURE OF THE LAW

by

Eric H. W. Voegelin, Dr. rer. Pol.

Professor of Government

Louisiana State University

Temporary edition exclusively for the use of
students registered in the course in Jurisprudence
(Law 112) at the Louisiana State University Law School.

Louisiana State University Law School

Baton Rouge, Louisiana

1957

CONTENTS

PROLOGUE

An inquiry concerning the nature of the law is burdened with suspicions about its feasibility, for the classic philosophers, Plato and Aristotle, had no philosophy of law. The problems that are treated in our modern legal theory under this head appeared in Plato under such titles as "justice" or "the true order of the polis," and in Aristotle as parts of the *episteme politike* with its subdivisions into ethics and politics. Hence, anyone who has some confidence in the acumen and competence of the two thinkers will be worried, at the outset of such an inquiry, by the thought that perhaps the law does not have a nature. Since the only reason for a thing not to have a nature is its lack of ontological status—the fact that it is not a self-contained, concrete thing in any realm of being—there arises the unpleasant question whether the law exists.

If Plato and Aristotle should prove right—if the law indeed is not a thing with a nature—formidable questions would arise with regard to the historical circumstances under which the illusion of the law as a thing with ontological status could form. But I do not want to anticipate. The questions of a philosophical inquiry must emerge from the analysis itself; they must not be introduced from the outside, through glances at authority however worthy. No more than a warning is intended that the analysis may not run smoothly and that the results may be unexpected.

The inquiry itself will start, without improper side-glances, from the phenomena of law as they present themselves in the contemporary horizon of our everyday knowledge, from the everyday language in which lawyers talk about the law, and from the questions arising at the surface of the phenomena through the language in everyday use.

I
THE VALID ORDER

Since everyone talks about "the law" as if it were an object of common knowledge, it will be proper to agree with the assumption and to begin the analysis with an observation that will lead to the question of nature or essence.

§ 1. Essence

The law, though we speak of it in the singular as if there were only one law, appears in a plurality of legal orders accepted as valid in a corresponding plurality of societies. Moreover, the contents of the several legal orders are not identical. A knowledge of American law will be of little use in a trial before a French judge; and even a thorough knowledge of the law of property in one of the forty-eight American states, while certainly helpful, by itself will be insufficient to decide a case in any one of the other states.

Before entering into the analysis of the observation, we must establish its analytical legitimacy as distinguished from its truth. The observation is true as a whole and in its parts, but it is not a random observation; it has been constructed carefully to make everyday language transparent for the problem of essence. A critic well might argue that a lawyer, when he speaks of "the law," usually will have in mind the concrete legal order in which he happens to be interested professionally and not "the law" that becomes manifest in the plurality of concrete legal orders; and the argument of the critic would be well taken. Nevertheless, it would not be an argument in the analysis but only an additional observation of phenomena on the level of everyday knowledge. On this level, indeed, "the law" can refer either to the single legal order or to "the law" in the sense that the critic on this same level would call with disgust "metaphysical."

This correctly observed equivocal use of "the law" will furnish the starting point for another line of analysis concerning the problem that the positive law of a society carries overtones of aspiration toward, if not realization of, a "higher law." This question of a "higher law," however, cannot be raised at the beginning of the inquiry, because the unfolding of its implications requires some clarity with regard to the question of whether law has an essence. The analytical legitimacy of the initial observation, as distinguished from its truth, is dependent on the order in which problems arise in the analysis; it is not affected by an equally true alternative observation about phenomena that partly overlap with those of the first observation.

The distinction between the truth and the analytical legitimacy of the observation, besides having its relevance for the theory of science, has its practical importance for the understanding of contemporary legal theory. A good deal of the confusion there is caused by the pitting of alternative phenomenal observations against one another. The distressing result is that, under the name of "theory," generalizations from preanalytical partial observations take the place of analysis.

Whereas the legitimacy of the initial observation can be demonstrated only through its role in the unfolding analysis, it has been secured sufficiently for the present against argument on the phenomenal level. To return to the analysis, let us recall the first sentence of the initial observation: the law, though we speak of it in the singular as if there were only one law, appears in a plurality of legal orders accepted as valid in a corresponding plurality of societies. This sentence suggests that "the law" is something like an essential aggregate of rules, a species or form, individuated in a plurality of legal orders, in the manner in which a biological species is individuated in a plurality of specimens. If this were the case, the search for the nature of the law could be conducted by comparing as many legal orders as possible, with a view to finding the rules that they have in common. If an aggregate of rules common to all legal orders were to be found, it could be considered the essence of the law, and the rules of varying contents could be considered nonessential properties of the individuals of the species "legal order." Classifications of this "botanical" type may lead one astray, however, and a search for essence is not completed until the analysis has "dissolved" the phenomena into concepts.

At this juncture, however, we need not go into the niceties of complete or incomplete, of imperfect or perfect analysis, for the rest of the initial observation [that the contents of the several legal orders are not identical] suggests that the relation of species and individuation does not apply to the case of the legal order understood as an aggregate of valid rules. In contrast to the manner in which variations of size among the individuals of an animal species can be distinguished as individual properties having nothing to do with its essential characteristics, "the law" in the sense of a concrete legal order—"the law" in which a lawyer is interested professionally—does not allow a distinction between essential rules and rules to be neglected as nonessential. In the law of the professional lawyer every rule is "essential" if it has a bearing on his case, even though the particular rule does not occur in any other known legal order.

The obstacle to a distinction between essential and nonessential rules is that quality of the legal rule to which we refer as its "validity." In a comparative study of legal orders understood as aggregates of legal rules (if anyone should undertake such a study with the purpose of finding the nature, or essence, of the law), a particular rule might be classified as a nonessential oddity occurring only in one lonely instance. Yet within its own order the rule would be "valid," and no lawyer would consider its validity impaired by the singularity of its occurrence. On the surface of the phenomena that have entered the observation, therefore, validity rather than essence seems to be the category under which "the law" must be approached.

Has the analysis, then, come off to a wrong start, if it looked for essence where it should have looked for validity? Certainly not, for analysis is the search for essence, and it will have reached its goal only when the preanalytical experience of phenomena is dissolved into concepts referring to an essence. If, on the occasion of this first step, the analysis stumbles over the problem of validity, the initial observation is defective, not the analysis. Perhaps, as we already suspected, the law as an aggregate of valid rules is not a thing with a nature. But we cannot let matters rest with this suspicion. It would be against common sense to assume that our preanalytical experience of the law is an illusion, even though the assumption that it is a thing with an ontological status of its own may be such an illusion. The law certainly is something, even if it should prove to be only a fragment of a more comprehensive entity. The difficulties of the moment do not spell the failure of the analysis, but, if properly thought through, will become the incentive for its advancement.

Two corollaries, in conclusion, will help clear the path by eliminating formally the two erroneous constructions that suggested themselves in this first phase of the analysis:

1. The problem of the essence of the law becomes baffling when we are confronted with a validity that permeates the legal order so completely that no nonessential elements are left. If the analysis were to stop at this point, one could find a theoretical construction that would satisfy the situation. We could assume that "the law" is not a genus individuated into species by the legal orders of concrete societies, but that all the rules of all the orders are equally of the essence of "the law" and form the only specimen of a vast species. The philosophical analysis of "the law" then would be reduced to a catalog of the orders and rules that compose this vast species. Such a construction, however, does not commend itself.

We know from everyday experience that a considerable number of legal orders have certain typical features in common, such as civil law, criminal law, commercial law, administrative law, the corresponding procedural laws, and so forth. As we shall see, the construction, if adopted, would prevent the exploration of typical structures in the legal order that do not come into view as long as the law is conceived as nothing but an aggregate of valid rules. The initial observation, thus, is fragmentary in that it brings into view only a small segment of the phenomena of law; and a construction adequate only to a small segment of our experience of the law, but pretending to be an exhaustive description of the "nature of the law," must be discarded as erroneous.

Caution is indicated, nevertheless, for the observation, though fragmentary, was true, and its construction of the law as a vast species, even if erroneous, may still contain some grain of that truth. Every legal rule really is valid within its own order; there is something to the conception of the law as a vast species consisting of a single specimen, though at the present we are not prepared to explore what that something is.

2. If the preceding construction, though it has to be eliminated for the reasons given, at least satisfies the problem of the valid

rules at this stage, then the earlier construction of the problem of essence certainly is wrong. The attempt to find the nature of the law by comparing several legal orders, with the hope of finding the essence as a recurrent aggregate of legal rules, must be abandoned as senseless. Even if such a recurrent aggregate could be found (though no one has found it yet), it would have no cognitive value, for we know through our everyday experience of the law that the validity of every single rule in the concrete order is somehow "of the essence of the law"—whatever that phrase may turn out to mean when submitted to further analysis. This prima facie element of essence must not be sacrificed to a construction that transfers the model of the biological sciences to the case of the law, which obviously has a quite different ontological structure.

The encyclopedic approach to a philosophy of law, that is, the attempt to determine the essence of the law by comparing a plurality of legal orders, is not new. It made its first appearance in the sophistic period, in the fifth century B.C. In his dialogue *Protagoras*, Plato presents the sophist Hippias as engaged in this attempt.

§ 2. Substance and Existence

The analytical attack on the problem of essence has been discomfited for the present. If we must reject the construction of a single vast species of all valid rules of all legal orders as indicating the essence of the law, we are thrown back on the concrete legal orders as the units of observation. Furthermore, if we must reject also the distinction between essential and nonessential rules within "the law" understood as an aggregate of valid rules, the inquiry into the nature of the law has reached an impasse. We must regain the momentum of the analysis through a return to the preanalytical experience of the law.

Since the validity of the law seems to be the source of the trouble, it will be advisable to cast around for our everyday knowledge about the validity of a legal order and its component rules. We will not look for a definition, to be sure, for definitions come at the end of an analysis, not at its beginning. What interests us now is precisely the everyday language that has not yet suffered from analytical refinements, the language in which things still make sense.

Only from the everyday language of lawyers, from the phenomenal surface of their usage, can we expect guidance toward the solution of our problems.

On this everyday level, we speak of legal rules duly enacted in statutory form, as for instance in an act of Congress, as valid rules of law. Before they were enacted, they were not valid; if they are in conflict with earlier statutes, the rules enacted at the earlier point in time will be invalid; if a later enactment should conflict with the present one, the rules that have become valid through the present enactment will be invalid. *Lex posterior derogat priori*— the later law invalidates the earlier one. And so forth.

From this complex of everyday knowledge, generally accepted as true among lawyers, more than one line of analysis can start, but we cannot follow them all at once. There is, for instance, the language of "enactment," of "acts of Congress," on which the validity of the rule seems to depend. The problem raised by this language will be deferred for later treatment. For the present we shall concentrate on the validity that comes and goes, that can be made to appear and disappear in time. The legal order, consisting of such valid rules, seems to have a time dimension; it seems to be an entity, after all, that exists in time. Perhaps the element of validity that proved an obstacle to the clarification of the law's essence will be of help in determining the law's manner of existence. Whatever may be the outcome of the attack on the problem of existence, perhaps it will make the problem of essence more tractable.

We shall start from the everyday assumption that legal orders do exist. While some rules in a legal order lose their validity, other rules become valid. There is an income and outgo of valid rules. The legal order changes, but it does not change in all of its parts at once; there remains, from one change to another, an unchanged corpus of rules sufficiently large to retain the identity of the order. The legal order of the moment does not give way to a new one, but it "changes." The problem of a thing preserving its identity while suffering changes in time does not seem to be different in the case of the legal order than it is in instances of things in other realms of being. A rock may be eroded by wind and rain, but we recognize it as the same rock as long as the changes are slow enough; if, however, under some impact, the rock splits into several parts, we are inclined to speak of the parts as separate rocks, even though we know about their connection with the former larger rock. When plants or animals grow and wither and, over a period of time, through metabolism, change completely the material composition of their organism, we speak of changes in the same plant or animal as long as the organic form is retained; but if the organic form decomposes through death, we no longer speak of the resultant processes as changes in the individual. The case of the legal order is similar to the ones just described—or so it seems, at least.

Against this everyday assumption, however, we must oppose the results that have been secured by the first step of the analysis. The legal order seems to be valid through and through, and validity, as we said, is "of the essence of the law." We cannot distinguish between essential and nonessential rules, as we can between essential and nonessential changes; nor can we gloss over the income and outgo of valid rules by comparison with the changes in things in other realms of being. The case of the law must be treated on its own merits. If we assume a legal order to be an aggregate of valid rules, we must ask the question anew: What happens to the legal order if any of its component rules is invalidated by a later law? Is the legal order, after the invalidation of one of its component parts, still the same entity as before, only slightly changed; or does every elimination of rules from, or addition of rules to, the aggregate create a new legal order? The answer is inevitable: if the legal order is identified as an aggregate of valid rules, every aggregate that differs with regard to its component parts from any other aggregate must be considered a different individual of the species "legal order" (suspending for the moment all questions concerning species and individuation). Every time Congress enacts a statute, the result will be a new legal order; and if Congress is busy, there will be the spectacle of several legal orders succeeding one another in the course of a single day.

No lawyer will accept this verdict as final. He will insist on his everyday language, in which the law changes in this or that respect through a new statute, while the identity of the legal order is not impaired by the entrance or exit of a number of valid rules. In face of this insistence, however, the philosopher too will have to be insistent. The verdict, indeed, is final because it is analytically necessary. No compromise is possible. We can find the way out of this conflict only by recognizing that in our everyday experience we know about a legal order that is *not* an aggregate of legal rules but a sequence of such aggregates.

In order to push the analysis ahead, we must introduce another preanalytical phenomenon of law. Now we must study the phenomenal circumstances that, on the everyday level, induce the language of the law [legal order] that changes.

One of these phenomena is, of course, the already-mentioned gradual entrance and exit of rules into a body of law that remains constant in its bulk, which suggested the analogy with changing things in other realms of being. The analogy, however, at least on this superficial level, has proved unworkable. One could, then, try to penetrate more deeply into the analogous instances in order to find out with more precision what, in these instances, induces the notion that a thing may remain the same while undergoing changes in time. The instance of the rock will not be much help for this purpose. Rocks are notoriously tough, and nothing is so difficult to understand as the nature of a dumb rock—as knows any philosopher who has tried. Organisms are much more amenable. Usually there are morphological constants that will permit a first grip on the nature of the individual; and with the advancement of genetics, a high degree of etiological understanding of the phenotypical constants becomes possible. The idea of finding in the legal order something like an organic form is at least suggestive, but the prospects do not look good, for both the distinction between essential and nonessential features and the relation between constant form and changing substance already have run into the obstacle of validity. The legal order that consists of a succession of aggregates of valid rules would have to contain a factor that we have not yet discovered.

The lawyer on the preanalytical level will be most eager to furnish the missing factor, and perhaps he will wonder why it was not introduced into the analysis long ago. The answer, though its simplicity will prove deceptive, is obvious: a series of aggregates is considered one legal order if the elements of the series are created successively by a constant procedure—in our American case, by the procedure provided by the Constitution. The constant procedure, while not an organic form present in the aggregates of rules produced by it, nevertheless will furnish the link between them.

The answer sounds convincing at first hearing, but as soon as one considers the notion of validity in relation to the legal order considered as a series of aggregates, one will have misgivings that the solution to the problem has been found. To be sure, at any given time there exists an aggregate of valid rules even under the new concept of legal order; but what has become of the rules that no longer are valid or "in force," as we say, but yet belong to the legal order in the new sense of a succession of aggregates held together by procedure? Into which limbo of nonvalidity have they disappeared? And if we must ask this question with regard to rules that at one time have been valid, must we not also ask the question, from which paradise of the unborn are the present rules drawn into validity? This latter question must be asked especially because in the expression *de lege ferenda* [law-in-the-making], legal practice possesses a term for the discussion of rules that are not valid parts of the present legal order but are being considered for reception as such parts.

The legal order in the second sense, thus, is composed of rules both valid and nonvalid; it has a clear time structure of a present of validity, with a past dimension of rules that have been valid, and a future dimension of rules that possibly will become valid. As appears from this language, moreover, the past and future rules of the legal order are not invalid rules without further qualification. They do not include the past or future rules of other legal orders, or rules that are not valid in the present of the given order but valid in the present of other coexisting orders, or rules that spring from somebody's roaming imagination but are not valid rules in any legal order at any time. The nonvalid rules of a given legal order have a definite status as formerly valid rules or as rules *de lege ferenda* in relation to the order's own presently valid rules.

Obviously, the initial assumption of the law as an aggregate of valid rules is far too narrow in the light of these reflections. A philosophy of law, if it wants to make explicit the meanings contained in the preanalytical knowledge of law, must not restrict itself to a theory of positive law, that is, of the law valid at any given present of a legal order. The preanalytical knowledge and language of lawyers about their law extend beyond the crosscut of the positive law into areas of which we may speak provisionally, without further analytical clarification at the moment, as the history of law and the law-in-the-making. We may now recall the earlier construction of the law as the vast species consisting of all valid rules of all legal orders. Although we had to reject the construction, we cautioned that there might be "something" to it, and a part of that "something" now comes into view.

§ 3. The Zenonic Problem

The problems just adumbrated have a high degree of complexity. Before we can approach them, we must analyze a number of questions closer at hand. While these preliminary questions are simpler in structure, their analysis will reveal that recourse to the constant procedure provided by the Constitution as the link between aggregates of norms does not solve the question of the legal order as an identifiable entity existing in time. As the aggregates of rules follow one another in time, validity seems to become something like a spotlight moving along the series of aggregates. Each element of the series is touched by that light for a moment, only to sink back into the darkness of invalidity while the light moves on toward future aggregates not yet valid. The law becomes a flow of rules, none of them valid inherently, passing through the present of validity as through a narrow. Even these metaphors, however, though they transform the law into a flow of essentially nonvalid rules and reduce validity to a passing quality, are not yet radical enough in diminishing the existence of the law as a valid legal order. For the legal order does not consist only of the general rules enacted by statutes, which are usually "in force" over an appreciable period of time and lend their appearance of a not-yet-analyzed duration to the "validity" in common parlance; it consists also, and eminently so, of court decisions.

If now we remember that the court decision is the point at which "the law" becomes valid for the concrete case, and if we remember the aura of uncertainty that surrounds every serious litigation, we must admit that we never know what the aggregate of valid rules really is as long as the court has not handed down its decision in the concrete case. Once the court has reached its decision, the particular aggregate whose validity has become complete with the decision, and thereby incorporates the decision into itself, belongs already to the past. If, therefore, validity is "of the essence of the law," and if every aggregate of rules in the series called legal order belongs either to a past in which it is no longer valid or to a future in which it is not yet valid in the decisive concrete case, then "the law" seems to have disappeared altogether from the realm of existents.

The result is paradoxic in the technical sense of the Zenonic *paradoxa*. And it will be well to recall the structure of the paradox in order to find the way out of this new impasse. The plainest paradox is that of the runner: it is impossible for the runner to reach the goal because he has to pass through an infinity of points. A famous instance of the paradox is that of Achilles and the tortoise. Achilles, in pursuit of the tortoise, can never catch up with it. He has first to reach the point from which the tortoise started; when he reaches that point, he then has to reach the point at which the tortoise is now; and so forth *ad infinitum*. And you will recall other instances of the paradox, such as that of the flying arrow that stands still. All of these *paradoxa* have their origin in the attempt to describe the motion of a thing, continuously moving in continuous time, by means of the infinity of static points on a line representing time, on each of which points the thing is imagined at rest. The attempt will not succeed, however, for the succession of static points, however close we let them succeed one another, will never become the continuum of a thing in motion.

We can understand the present impasse of the analysis in terms of the Zenonic problems. We have understood the legal order, first, as an aggregate of valid rules and, second, as a series of such aggregates linked by constitutional procedure. The legal order in the first sense is the static point on a time dimension created by the constitutional procedure; and the legal order in the second sense is the continuum imagined as a series of static points on the line. The succession of the static points will never run together into the authentic continuum of a thing that really exists in time.

That is a distressing result, for philosophical analysis has the purpose of making explicit the sense contained in everyday knowledge; it does not have the purpose of making nonsense of it, not even if the nonsense has the intellectual elegance of a Zenonic *paradoxon.* Again we must return to the preanalytical experience for guidance, for the everyday experience is not proved to be an illusion if, in the course of its analysis, the object disappears from existence. The result rather provides reason to suspect that its premises were defective. We had assumed the legal order to be an aggregate of valid rules and then expanded the meaning to that of a series of such aggregates linked by constitutional procedure. Since these assumptions have led to the paradoxic result, the conclusion must be either that the legal order is not an aggregate of valid rules at all, or that the language of "rules" and "validity" contains meanings that have escaped us, or that the nature of the law cannot be determined unless the aggregates of valid rules are placed into contexts of everyday experience that hitherto have not come under observation.

The choice among these various conclusions will be narrowed down, at least to a degree, if we formulate the important intermediate result of this second phase of the analysis: no theory of law can be constructed, without running into the Zenonic paradox, if the theory is based on the assumption that a legal order is an aggregate of valid rules, or norms, and nothing but such an aggregate. The difficulty arises from the fact that a realm of meanings, such as the meanings of legal norms, has no time dimension. The meanings may refer to objects, events, and actions in time, but they themselves are not existents in time. The validity of a rule, its normative character, is part of its meaning, but it does not confer an ontological status on the rule. A theoretical construction that bases itself on the normative character of the rules is tied to the "static" character of their meaning and cannot break through to the continuum of existence in time.

This intermediate result, to be sure, is negative. Considering, nevertheless, the state of intellectual confusion in contemporary legal theory, the result itself, as well as the method by which it has been achieved, must not be underrated. The plethora of legal theories, the bewildering variety of positions in our time, is caused by the unwillingness to submit to analysis the partial verities that can be drawn in great numbers from the preanalytical experience of "the law." They are left at the stage of unanalyzed initial assumptions. Whenever, therefore, our analysis reveals the partial character of an assumption, not only have we advanced the inquiry concerning the nature of the law through revealing the necessity of further assumptions, but at the same time we have disposed of a considerable body of speculation and controversy that has grown around an unanalyzed partial "theory."

In the light of these reflections, finally, we must eliminate a line of theoretical construction that may look tempting at this second stage of the analysis. We have studied the legal order as the aggregate of valid rules and as the series of such aggregates. But what has become of the constitutional procedure that provided the link between the two phenomena? Is it not possible that the existence of the legal order in time, which could be found neither in the aggregates nor in their series, is to be found in the constitutional procedure? The idea is suggestive, but the attempt to push the analysis in this direction also will end in disappointment, for the constant procedure provided by the constitution must itself be described in terms of valid rules. A constitution in the material sense is the aggregate of rules concerning the organization, jurisdiction, and procedure of the supreme organs of government within a society. Again we are faced with an aggregate of rules. And as far as the existence of the legal order in time is concerned, nothing has been gained by the addition of the aggregate of constitutional norms to such aggregates as the civil or criminal law. The fact that a realm of meanings has no time dimension is not abolished by the specific contents of a set of rules. The timeless validity of the rule does not acquire existence in time simply because the content of the rule concerns a procedure in time. The restrictive formulations of the preceding paragraph, therefore, now must be supplemented by the understanding that the time dimension of a legal order cannot be established by moving upward or downward in a hierarchy of sub-aggregates linked by rules of procedure. The constitution may delegate legislative powers to organs of government; the legislative organs may create general rules and delegate further rule-making powers to courts and administrative agencies; and these lines of delegation may be articulated further by any number of intermediate lawmaking agencies. But with all these complications of the legal order in a modern state, no time dimension is gained. We still move in a realm of meaning, though this realm now has acquired the structure of a hierarchy of norms. No expansion of a legal theory to encompass a hierarchy of rules linked by procedure and delegation can avoid the Zenonic problem.

II
THE VALID ORDER AND THE SOCIAL CONTEXT

The analysis has explored the aggregate of valid rules under the categories of essence, substance, and existence. The result is negative. No thing with an ontological status could be found. The phenomena that proved insufficient as a basis for theoretical construction now must be supplemented by contextual phenomena that came into view more than once on the margin of the analysis but were disregarded then in the interest of its orderly conduct.

§ 1. The Hierarchy of Valid Rules. The Lawmaking Process. The Order of Society at Large

On the occasion of the first observation, we noted that a lawyer, when he speaks of "the law," does not necessarily mean the law [as a species] that is individuated in the plurality of legal orders, but rather the concrete law in which he is interested professionally. That law is for every lawyer the law of his country on all levels of centralization and decentralization, such as federal law, state law, and local ordinances. In this sense we speak of American, English, or French law as the legal order of certain countries. The specific country emerges as the case of a society that "has" a legal order, and the law emerges as something inherent in a society. Then, on the occasion of the second observation, we used language that indicated the existence of an organization for the purpose of "making" the rules that, after they have been made, are parts of the aggregate of legal rules. We spoke of legal rules created by acts of Congress, of decisions made by courts and administrative agencies, and so forth.

It seems we can advance the analysis, therefore, by turning from the rules as a self-contained realm of meaning to the society in which human beings, under the title of organs of government, make the law, presumably with a purpose. That is not to say that the rules, the aggregates of rules, and the problem of their validity have to be abandoned as irrelevant. On the contrary, we shall see the problem of validity recur with new complications on this further state of the analysis. The sense that the enumerated phenomena make in our everyday experience, nevertheless, is connected closely with the social context in which they appear: a court decision is not merely a valid rule but lays down with social consequences what the law is in the concrete case under trial. The general rules on the statutory level provide the types into which judges and administrative officers have to fit their individual decisions in concrete cases. Constitutional rules, on the other hand, provide the procedures and the range of powers for the organs of government that will formulate the general types, which in their turn will be applied to concrete cases on the level of individual decisions. The elaborate hierarchy of subaggregates in the legal order (of which we have indicated no more than representative instances) is infused with the purpose of particularizing "the law" for concrete relations among human beings.

The language of "purpose," however, must be used with caution. It would be easy to derail at this juncture into the "purposes of the law" in the sense of variegated, not-too-well defined "ideals" propounded in this or that variety of teleological jurisprudence. At the present we are concerned, not with the specific purposes of a legislative measure, but with the manner in which legal rules are fitted phenomenally into the social context, with the manner in which they partake of existence even though they do not have autonomous existence. Moreover, this manner of participation is much more intricate than the language of means-end relations would suggest. Yet, the term *purpose* is indispensable, as we shall see, in order to stress the peculiarly weighted relationship between "the law" and the society that has it.

The intricate pattern in which legal rules interweave with social reality will become apparent through a brief consideration of the hierarchy of rules and aggregates of rules. One can, to be sure, consider the legal order with its hierarchical structure as a realm of meanings. The contents of a statute can be accorded the rank of valid rules in a legal order if the statute was enacted by the competent legislative organ in accordance with the procedural rules of the constitution, and if, furthermore, its contents are not in conflict with such substantive rules as a written constitution may provide. The contents of an executive order may be considered valid if the order rests on proper authorization by a statute that itself is not unconstitutional—and so forth, through the legal hierarchy down to the ultimate, individual decisions. The result of the examination can be set forth in the form of a treatise, for instance, on the valid civil law of a country, drawing for its "sources" on constitutional rules, statutory rules, judicial decisions, et cetera.

In such a "dogmatic" [doctrinal] treatment of the law, however, the actual intertwining of the legal rules with the social process of their making will not become explicit; for the legislative action required to produce the valid rules of the statute is itself neither a constitutional nor a statutory rule, but a series of actions of particular human beings. The same is true on the level of individual decisions. The deliberations of a jury and the pronouncement of a verdict, for example, are not the verdict itself, and the reasoning process of the judge and his pronouncement of sentence are not the sentence as a valid rule. The levels of valid rules in the hierarchy of a legal order, therefore, not only are distinguishable as such by the logic of procedural delegation, but also are separated from each other in social reality through the interspersed acts of their specification.

These acts of lawmaking on the various levels, moreover, are not merely acts in a social sphere of nonlegal character but partake of the "nature of the law" inasmuch as they themselves must have legal character in order to produce valid rules. Not everyone's declaration of general rules constitutes a statute with a legally valid content. A statute will result only when specific men in a specific pattern of action, that is, when members of a legislature constituted and acting in the form provided by the constitution, agree on certain rules. The same argument applies to individual decisions of courts and administrative agencies. A social reality of valid actions dovetails with the law as an aggregate of valid rules. Certain acts of human beings produce valid rules if they are recognizable as lawmaking acts in the light of other rules, and these in their turn are valid rules insofar as they are formulated through acts recognizable as lawmaking acts under still other rules, and so forth.

The notion of a hierarchy of valid rules, thus, must be expanded into a lawmaking process in which rules and rule-making acts alternate. This process, finally, flows into the vast reality of the society that "has" the law that is made in the process. Even this vast reality beyond the lawmaking process in the technical sense, however, has a mode of partaking of the law. Although we do not speak of businessmen as lawmakers, their contracts will have the force of law between them if drafted in such form that courts will recognize their binding force and attach certain consequences to their nonfulfillment. The rules of the law of contracts provide types of agreements, not only for the judge who has to decide a case when it comes before him, but also for the persons who want to enter into a contractual agreement. The contracting parties indeed make valid rules, binding on themselves in the sense that their own future actions can be understood as fulfillment or nonfulfillment of the agreement. These lawmaking actions of the members of the society who live under the law are so frequent and so important that professional assistance in such actions forms a major segment of lawyers' business. The relations among human beings in a society, thus, to a large extent have legal structure.

The legal character of social reality, however, is even more pervasive than it appears to be if we consider nothing more than the specific rules created by members of the society for themselves. The law, for instance, not only provides types for acts that, by conforming to a prescribed pattern, acquire the character of lawmaking acts; it also provides types for acts that, by conforming to yet other patterns, acquire the character either of lawful acts or of "violations" of the law. In the latter case, human conduct becomes relevant legally precisely when it is "illegal" in the sense of a delict in civil or criminal law. The man who does nothing at all to attract the attention of "the law," favorably or unfavorably, is the man whose conduct partakes most thoroughly of the nature of the law. By implication, then, the man who does not violate the law is the man who observes it. This implication is made explicit in our everyday experience of law and society, when to the lawbreaker we oppose "the law-abiding citizen."

In this respect, everyday language is especially illuminating, because it has a rich vocabulary for the types of conduct intermediate between law-abiding and lawbreaking. We speak of men who observe the letter of the law while violating its spirit; who cut corners; who are smart enough not to get caught; who know how to keep out of trouble and not tangle with the courts; who find loopholes in the law; who have smart lawyers for the purpose of using, or rather misusing, the law of evidence to obtain an acquittal, though obviously the crime was committed; and so forth. All these everyday categories reveal a thorough understanding of a relation between law and society so intimate that the whole existence of man in society is pervaded with "law," even if a specific relation of legal relevance between a type of action and a type provided by the legal order does not exist.

§ 2. The Law as the Substance of Order. The Lawmaking Process as the Instrument for Securing the Substance

The phenomena just introduced do not merely raise one or two further questions but open up a whole field of inquiry. Only one problem, however, will be singled out for present examination: the equivocal use of "the law" in the sense of valid rules made by organs of government and "the law" that somehow pervades the existence of man in society. What is preserved in this pale equivocation of our everyday language is the profound insight, rarely to be found in contemporary legal theory, that "the law" is the substance of order in all realms of being. As a matter of fact, the ancient civilizations usually have in their languages a term that signifies the ordering substance pervading the hierarchy of being, from God, through the world and society, to every single man. Such terms are the Egyptian *maat*, the Chinese *tao*, the Greek *nomos*, and the Latin *lex* [*ius?*]. The Egyptian *maat*, for instance, signifies the order of the gods who, by virtue of their *maat*, create the order of the cosmos. Within this cosmic order, the term then applies specifically to the order of the realm of Egypt, which order is created by virtue of the divine *maat* that lives in the Pharaoh. From the Pharaoh that *maat* streams through the social body, mediated by the royal administration and the hierarchy of officers, down to the judge who decides the individual case. Since the mediation of *maat* requires its understanding and intelligent articulation, the term acquires the meaning of "truth" about order; and since the knowledge of that truth is not a monopoly of the administration, the law as administered can be measured by the common knowledge about the truth of order, and the subjects can protest vehemently against deviations from the *maat* and criticize the conduct of officials.

24

The Egyptian usage will illuminate the problem at hand, for the compact symbolism of the *maat* shows that behind the equivocations of our everyday language lies the experience of a substance that pervades the order of being, of which the order of society is a part. As far as the order of society is concerned, the substance pervades the whole of it, including that part which today we differentiate as the lawmaking process. The law is something that is essentially inherent in society, though the manner of this inherence is complicated by the fact that it must be secured, as we shall say cautiously, by organized human action, the type of action of which we speak as the lawmaking process.

Such an assumption will satisfy the everyday language of "the lawbreaker" and "the law-abiding citizen" considerably better than the alternative constructions built on the isolated phenomenon of the lawmaking process. If, for example, the criminal law with its types of crimes is taken in isolation, and especially if the criminal law is couched in the form of if-laws, it can be, and indeed has been, constructed as a body of rules that order courts to respond with certain actions—called trial, sentence, and execution—to actions that conform to the "if" part of the law. The legal order, under this construction, would not prohibit murder, theft, and so forth, but would only attach certain consequences to these types of action, leaving it to the discretion of the citizen to avoid or to seek the sanctions. The normative character, the "Thou shalt not," would have been removed from the substantive rules of criminal law, and it would make no sense to speak of a crime as an illegal action, or of the man who commits it as a lawbreaker. In our everyday experience of the law, then, the reason why certain consequences, understood as "punishments," should be attached to certain types of action, understood as "crimes," would not be a question to be examined in a philosophy of law. Issues of this type would belong to a realm of "moral" purposes beyond the law. The meaning of "law-abiding citizen" also would evaporate, for nothing such a citizen does could be classified as legally relevant in terms of actions falling under types provided in the aggregate of valid rules.

Against this construction lies the same argument as that against the impasse of the Zenonic paradox: the purpose of analysis is not to make nonsense of our preanalytical knowledge about law, but rather to make its sense explicit. Hence, we must prefer the assumption that the lawmaking process makes sense as an instrument for securing the substance of order that inheres essentially in society. The assumption, moreover, commends itself especially because the legal order in the sense of the aggregate of valid rules rarely is couched in the normative language of the "Thou shalt" or "Thou shalt not." The written law usually describes types of facts, events, and behaviors that become legally relevant through the other types of facts, events, and behaviors of organs of government that ensue in case of conformity or nonconformity to the first class of types. That the chain of types is constructed with the purpose of securing order in social relations is not made explicit necessarily in the text of a law, though the so-called intention of the lawgiver may be stated explicitly in "preambles" to the law. In the major modern codifications, however, the intention is presupposed, and the legal technique of the codemaker is concentrated on the task of constructing types that will realize the intention with a maximum of probability. The commonly used language of legal rules or norms, therefore, always must be understood as the text of the law read in the light of its normative intention. It is possible, in principle, to construct an entire legal order through definitions and propositions without ever using normative vocabulary.

In summary of these reflections it can be said: the lawmaking process partakes of the nature of the law inasmuch as it serves the purpose of securing the substance of order in society; and the order in society is the area in which we have to search for the nature of the law.

§ 3. Theoretical Constructions of the Relation

The relations just indicated have motivated a number of constructions in the philosophy of law. The principal types are the following:

1. In Plato and Aristotle the accent lies on the substance of order in society, specifically on the order of the Hellenic polis. The inquiry into the true order of the polis is the philosopher's principal task. Specific rules are formulated under the aspect that they articulate the true order in society and, if enacted, will secure it. The lawmaking process is studied under the aspect whether its organization will result in rules that will secure the true order.

2. The lawmaking process moves into the center of interest with the genesis of the modern national state. In the struggle with the authorities of Church and Empire, of Roman Law and the Estates, the governments of the rising national states assert the supremacy of the state in the making of the law. The prince, as the representative of the state, becomes the sovereign lawmaker. All valid law emanates from him, either directly or from agents to whom he has delegated lawmaking authority.

Nevertheless, while the accents have shifted, the lawmaking process is not yet self-contained. The awareness remains that the sovereign lawmakers have to secure a substance of order that is not of their making. This is the type of construction represented by Bodin in the sixteenth century. The law is recognized under its two aspects of a hierarchy of valid rules and a hierarchy of lawmaking authorities. The hierarchy of valid rules has as its top stratum the divine and natural law; under this stratum move the statutes of the prince; then follows customary law insofar as it is not in conflict with the royal statutes; next come the decisions of the magistrates, moving within the law as fixed by the higher strata; and at the bottom come the legal transactions of the subjects—their buying and selling, their labor contracts, marriages, wills, and so forth. The hierarchy of lawmaking authorities, in reverse order, begins with the subjects, rises through magistrates and the king, and culminates in God.

In the seventeenth century, however, the link of the sovereign lawmaking process with an autonomous substance of order is notably weakened in the construction of Hobbes. Hobbes reduces the substance of order to the postulate of peace within the community. Whether or not the resulting order manifests the Judaeo-Christian substance, still envisaged by Bodin, is put at the discretion of the Sovereign. Whether the Commonwealth of England will be Christian or not becomes a matter not of substantive order but of historical accident.

3. With the progress of secularism and the disintegration of philosophy in the nineteenth and twentieth centuries, the lawmaking process achieves complete autonomy, *i.e.*, its theorists remove from legal theory the question of substantive order. Moreover, the theorists display a tendency to split the lawmaking process itself into two components, the valid rules and the acts of their creation,

and to make each of the components independently the basis of theoretical construction. The result is a parallel development of normative and sociological jurisprudence.

4. The representative case of normative jurisprudence is Kelsen's "Pure Theory of Law." In this theory, the lawmaking process acquires the monopoly of the title "law," as Kelsen blends norms and legally relevant acts into one normative realm. Kelsen's hierarchy culminates in a hypothetical basic norm that orders the members of society to behave in conformity with the norms deriving ultimately from the constitution. The power structure articulated in the constitution is the origin of the legal order, surmounted by the hypothetical basic norm only to make the highest ordering acts intelligible as acts in conformity with a norm, thereby closing the normative system.

The law and the state, then, according to Kelsen, are two aspects of the same normative reality. Since the hypothetical basic norm replaces the Bodinian divine and natural law as the top stratum of the hierarchy, the problems of substantive order are eliminated. Whatever power establishes itself effectively in a society is the lawmaking power, and under its hypothetical norm, whatever rules it makes are the law. The classic questions of true and untrue, of just and unjust order do not belong in the science of law or, for that matter, in any science at all. For the only science of society that Kelsen admits by the side of normative jurisprudence is a "sociology" defined as a science that is concerned with human actions and their causal relations. The whole area of the Aristotelian *episteme politike* is not science and, therefore, does not deserve the attention of a theorist.

5. In the case of attempts to use lawmaking acts as the basis of theoretical construction, it is difficult to single out a representative system. Here we are faced rather with a large variety of attempts at a "sociology" of law. According to their interests, the authors concentrate either on the constitutional and legislative processes, or on the court decisions at various levels, or on the behavior of the general public and its subgroups. A rich vocabulary of legislative purposes and legal functions signifies the manifold relations between human beings and the order of the society in which they live—a vocabulary of domestic peace, welfare, and social security; of freedom and property; of class and group interests; of pro-

tection of the weak; of adjustment, deterrence, prevention, and re-habilitation; of lawful and unlawful, social and unsocial behavior; and so forth.

What the terms of this class, and the sociological theories in which they occur, have in common is their preanalytical character. The inquiry is not advanced to the point where the criteria of true order in the philosophical sense come into view. In their aggregate, they reflect the same state of philosophical disintegration that is manifest in the normative jurisprudence. The nature of the law as the substantive order of society will not become the object of analysis if the inquiry stops short at the observation of such phenomena as the behavior of judges, the demands of pressure groups, the ideologies of political movements, the psychology of conformity or delinquency, the need of legislative and judicial reform, and so forth.

III
THE COMPLEX OF ORDER

The law in the sense of an aggregate of valid rules must be placed in the social context of the process in which it is created; and the lawmaking process in turn must be placed in the context of the society that secures its substantive order by means of this process. The whole complex is one unit of meaning, one entity. The term *law*, therefore, will change its meaning as it is used to signify either the whole or only one part of the complex. The equivocations caused by this situation can be avoided only through an artificial terminology at considerable variance with everyday usage—a procedure not to be recommended. Therefore, I shall introduce conceptual distinctions as they become necessary, with appropriate cautions when using conventional vocabulary.

§ 1. Structure, Continuity, and Identity of the Complex

At the present juncture such a caution is necessary, for we must distinguish between 1) "the law" in the sense of legal rules and the lawmaking process and 2) "the law" in the sense of the substantive order of society. We shall speak of the two areas of the total complex as its legal and social areas or sides, with the understanding that the whole complex is the entity whose nature we are exploring when we are in search of the "nature of the law." The terminological narrowing of "legal" does not imply an essential narrowing, for we consider it established that the legal order as an aggregate of rules has no ontological status and, consequently, neither essence nor existence.

In the structure of this entity as a whole we can discern two essential tensions: 1) there is a tension between the substantive order of society and the lawmaking process insofar as the organized process of making the law is apparently the inevitable means for keeping the substantive order in existence; and 2) there is a tension between the substantive order of society as it exists empirically and a true substantive order of which the empirical order falls short.

At present we shall deal only with the first of these tensions, the orientation of the legal order as a means for achieving substantive order in society. Of this rather complex relationship, moreover, we shall single out first the weighting of the relation toward the social side of the complex. The question of the valid legal order now must be reexamined. Having found in society the something that attaches the weight of existence in time to the legal order, we must ask again: What do we mean by "the law" when we speak of American or Italian law, or of the history of French civil or administrative law? Obviously we do not mean merely the aggregate of valid rules or the series of aggregates, but we let flow into our language a component of meaning that stems from the social side.

The peculiar weighting effect of the social side will become both apparent and intelligible if we reflect on certain border questions of constitutional law.

If the legal order is understood as the aggregate of valid rules or as a series of aggregates, all component parts of the order derive their validity, through the mediating links of procedural rules, from the constitution in the material sense. The legal order is constituted as an identifiable unit of meaning by the rules concerning the procedure of its creation. The apparent clarity of the construction, of course, is disturbed by the previously raised question concerning the status of rules that once were valid under the constitution but are not now, and those that are not valid now but will be in the future—but that question we still must leave suspended. We shall rather reflect on the phenomenon of the so-called "changes" in the constitution itself, as well as on the provisions for its own amendment that it may contain.

On principle, to be sure, the same argument applies to the aggregate of constitutional rules as applies to all other subaggregates of valid rules: the aggregate does not "change" through the entrance or exit of rules, but it is transformed into a different aggregate. With the constitutional procedures, however, we have reached the top of the hierarchy of rules. There is no constitution above the constitution that would link a series of constitutional aggregates into one legal order in the manner in which the statutory subaggregates are linked by the constitution. We have arrived at the border at which the problem of validity no longer can be solved intrasystematically through regress to a procedurally higher aggregate of rules. We are faced with the phenomenon that the validity of the law has its origin in extralegal sources.

At this juncture, more than one line of analysis branches off. In the first place, the problem can be eliminated through a construction of the type that Kelsen has attempted with his hypothetical basic norm. The purpose of the construction is to top with a norm the processes in which the constitution has originated. The hypothetical norm confers legal validity on the constitution itself and closes the legal "system." This construction must be rejected as analytically senseless. It does not analyze anything but cuts off the inquiry into the nature of the law. In science we are interested in the study of reality, not in the construction of a "system" that precludes its study.

A second line opens with Bodin's differentiation of the hierarchy of the norms for the lawmaking process into divine and natural law. Here we reach indeed new areas of reality, that is, the sources of authority from which the law derives its validity. We shall not follow this path at present, however, but defer it for later exploration; for besides the authorities to which the symbols "divine and natural law" refer, there is a further source of authority, the authority of organized social power. Bodin takes this authority into account in his philosophy of law when he lets the prince derive his sovereign lawmaking power from his sword as well as from God. The "powers that be" confer validity on the law when they enact it, and they have the first claim to our attention because the power structure of a society is the reality that becomes legally articulate in the rules of the constitution in the material sense.

The rules of a constitution try to create a stable order for a society by placing the supreme ordering power in organs of government that represent the actual power articulation of the society. If the makers of the constitution have diagnosed the actual power articulation of the society correctly; if, further, they are good craftsmen and know how to give legal articulation to the power reality of their society; and if, finally, the power structure that has entered the constitution is a stable one, then the constitution will last. Setting aside questions of correct diagnosis and craftsmanship, the constitution will not last if the power structure is unstable. In that case more or less violent events will occur, and the constitutional rules will have to be adapted to the changing power structure through usage, interpretation, formal amendment, or complete replacement.

These phenomena of adaptation now give rise to questions concerning the identity of a legal order. If a country emerges from a revolution with a new constitution, created by procedures not provided by the previous constitution, one legal order has come to its end and a new one has emerged. If in the face of this phenomenon we adopt the construction of the law as an aggregate of valid rules deriving from the constitution, we shall arrive at the conclusion that with the new legal order a new "state" has been created, not identical with the old "state" under the previous constitution. Such constructions have indeed been attempted and carried to their logical conclusion: that the validity of a statute, though it has survived the revolution unchanged, does not derive from the old, but from the new, constitution. Regardless of the continuance of the main body of legal rules, a new legal order has been created when the constitutional continuity suffers revolutionary interruption. Special legal arrangement will have to be made to connect the new state with its predecessor, if that should prove desirable. Revolutionary governments frequently display sympathy for this construction, for it seems to give them the right to repudiate the debts incurred by the prerevolutionary government. The victims of such repudiation, on the contrary, if they have the power, will insist that revolutionary replacements of legal order do not abolish such obligations; that the society that has undergone the change in its power structure is still the same society; and that there is a continuity between the pre- and postrevolutionary governments provided by the continuity of society.

§ 2. Aristotle's Struggle with the Problem of Identity

Aristotle was plagued greatly by this class of problems. He applied to the polis the categories of form and substance, assuming the constitution, the *politeia*, to be the form. He had developed these categories when considering the natures of artifacts, organisms, and purposive action. Although suitable to these models, these categories created difficulties when applied to the polis. What was the substance of a society, if the constitution was its form? Was it the citizens? If so, who was a citizen? Was everyone to be counted as a citizen who was a permanent resident on the territory of the polis? But then slaves and medics would be citizens, and that usage would be in conflict with preanalytical, everyday language. Should a man be counted as a citizen only if he may participate in the governmental process, if not in higher office, then at least by voting in assembly? That definition, however, will run into the difficulty that not all poleis have the form of a democracy. In a tyranny or oligarchy not all free men will have the right to vote in assembly, though they will not lose, as a consequence, their status as citizens and sink to the rank of medics or slaves. Nevertheless, while admitting that the definition of the citizen as a man who participates in the governmental process suits a democracy better than other forms of government, Aristotle does not push the analysis further, because he wants to retain the governmental form, the constitution, as the form of the polis. Doing so, however, he must define the citizens, the substance that fills the forms, as persons who have a place and function within the form.

The construction, then, leads to the further difficulty of identifying a polis. If the constitution is the form of the polis, and if a thing is ontologically constituted by its form, what happens to a polis in the frequent revolutions in the Greek city-states of Aristotle's time? Is there a new polis every time the oligarchs overthrow the democrats, or vice versa? Or is Athens, in spite of the breaks in the continuity of its constitutional form, still Athens? Most importantly, does the polis act when an oligarchic government contracts a debt, or can such debts be repudiated by a succeeding democratic government because oligarchies represent only private interests and not the common good—an argument apparently very much in favor with the leaders of democratic factions? For Aristotle, the answers to questions of this nature depend on the answer to the ultimate question: Do we want to speak of a polis as the same polis as long as the people and its abode remain the same, in spite of the fact that the members of the polis are a flow of generations, a flow of human beings coming into existence and dying, and thus never are the same from day to day?

Aristotle is driving this argument, from the social side of order, toward the same Zenonic impasse toward which, at the beginning of this inquiry, we drove it from the side of the valid legal order. Society is an entity composed of human beings. If we try to identify society with its membership, then, because of its daily increase and decrease by births and deaths, we shall find no society with continuous existence in time, but a new society every day. The polis, therefore, must be defined in terms, not of human beings, but rather of citizens as the substance of its form; and the form will be the constitution. If the constitution is the same, the polis is the same regardless of the increase and decrease of its citizen substance. Aristotle ends the analysis with the assurance that none of this affects the question whether a polis should or should not pay its debts when the constitution, the *politeia*, changes. He leaves this question dangling, just as he leaves dangling the question of the status of the citizens under an oligarchic or tyrannical constitution in which they do not participate in the governmental process and, also, the question of the continuous existence of Athens through its numerous changes of constitution.

The Aristotelian arguments are of considerable interest for our analysis because in them we encounter again the Zenonic paradox. From the paradoxic impasse of the validity of legal rules, their aggregates, and the succession of aggregates, we sought refuge in society as the something that exists in time. Aristotle discovers society as a flow of human beings in time that never will congeal to the sameness of a society of any duration in time, and he seeks refuge in the constitution as the form that lasts while its substance, the citizens, changes in time. That is most distressing. The Aristotelian analysis seems to cut off our escape into society, and our analysis already has cut off the escape from society into the duration of the legal order that culminates in the constitution. Nevertheless, we need not despair. Aristotle was a master of analysis. If his results are unsatisfactory, his analysis at least reveals, as will every technically well-conducted analysis, the cause of the difficulty. The cause of the difficulty is the uncritical transfer of the categories of form and substance to realms of being for which they were not developed.

This transfer leads to difficulties not only in the politics of Aristotle but also in his psychology when he tries to construct a noetic form of the soul. It leads in turn to infinite difficulties in medieval scholastic anthropology and psychology, where the soul is used in speculation as the "form" of man. In the case at hand, the transfer prevents Aristotle from properly connecting his theory of the "form" of the polis (in *Politics III*) with his theory of the nature of the polis (*Politics I*). He insufficiently analyzes the problem of the lawmaking process culminating in the constitution, and he never clarifies at all the connection of this problem with the order of the polis that exists continuously in time and is to be secured by the lawmaking process, whether democratic or oligarchic at the top of the hierarchy. These observations should serve as a warning. We are dealing with a problem that baffled even an Aristotle. We must take the utmost care in watching every step of the analysis.

§ 3. The Border Questions of Constitutional Law

The sameness [continuity] of the legal order obviously is bristling with problems. We must fall back on the preanalytical phenomena in order to avoid misconstructions. We can derive some help in understanding the relations between the legal order and social reality from phenomenal situations in which revolutions in the power structure occur without a break in legal continuity. In the nineteenth and early twentieth centuries, for instance, the transition from an absolute to a representative constitutional monarchy was more than once effected by having the absolute monarch impose the constitution. In the case of such an octroi constitution, the question can be asked whether the resulting legal order derives its validity from the new constitution or from the decree of proclamation of the absolute monarch who imposes the constitution. The leaders of the political forces who exacted the concession from the monarch would derive the validity of the new constitution from the authority of the newly effective political powers. The monarch would be inclined to derive it from his own untouched authority and claim the right to revoke it, if necessary in the interest of the state, by virtue of his continuing authority. While the two sides thus might disagree on the political issue, they would agree that the validity of the legal order culminating in the constitution had something to do with the authority of political power in society. It is understandable, therefore, that the leaders of constitutionalist movements in the nineteenth century had little sympathy for the method of the octroi, for it created an equivocal situation with regard to the source of authority.

Further illuminating phenomena are provided by the oddities surrounding the policies of constitution-making in the German National Socialist revolution. Since "legality" has mass appeal in the mob psychology of the twentieth century, the National Socialist leadership took care to adapt the constitutional rules to the new power structure by means of the amendment procedures provided by the Weimar Constitution. (The same method had been used previously, at least for a time, by the Fascist government in Italy.) The result was a spate of monographs by German constitutional lawyers, some pleading that the Weimar Constitution was still in force, others pleading that the revolutionary change in the power structure had created a new constitution, the games of legality notwithstanding. In this instance, it became an even more burning issue whether the identity of the legal order was to be construed in terms of intrasystematic, procedural validity or in terms of the authority that emanated from the power structure of society.

An important phenomenon, finally, is furnished by the history of our own Constitution. The procedure by which the Constitution of 1789 was created had not been provided by the Articles of Confederation. In terms of procedural validity, the Philadelphia Convention was a revolutionary assembly and the continuity of the legal order had been broken. Nevertheless, while the term *revolution* ordinarily is used in connection with the events of 1776 and after, it is very little used in connection with the events of 1789—in spite of the fact that the constitutional continuity was broken and that not all the means for achieving ratification of the new

Constitution in the several states fell under the heads of sweetness and reason. The peculiarity will become intelligible if the whole period, from the beginning of the movement for independence to the making of the Constitution of 1789, is considered one social process in which the growing nation, winding its way through the difficulties of intercolonial and interstate relations and the labors of the war, gained its power physiognomy and, after the unsatisfactory experiments with the Continental Congress and the Articles of Confederation, at last found the Constitution that was valid and at the same time expressive of the authoritative power structure of the new nation. The genesis of the American Constitution in the events between 1776 and 1789 furnishes perhaps the finest object-lesson for the growth of authoritative power in a new society, accompanied as it was by superb craftsmanship in devising legal forms for the stable structure. The case is of special importance for our analysis, because the protraction of the social process and the manner in which the questions of legality and constitutionality are subordinated to the questions of creating and ordering the nation leave no doubt whatsoever on which side the weight of the complex phenomenon of law lies.

The variety of examples will have clarified at least one question concerning the nature of the law. The legal order in the sense of an aggregate of valid rules is not an independent object of inquiry at all. It is part of a larger phenomenon that includes, among other things, the efforts of human beings to establish order in a concrete society. The larger phenomenon, furthermore, is not a composite of neatly separable parts, such as the valid rules and the social processes. The actual power structure with its authority enters the validity of the rules themselves. Controversies can arise, therefore, whether the validity of a given aggregate of rules should be construed under the aspect either of legality or of political authority.

The peculiar relation between the two components becomes especially clear in the case of conflict. Under ordinary circumstances, we may say, the amendment procedures built into a constitution will be sufficient to absorb the minor changes in the actual power structure and to provide the continuum of validity that expresses, on the side of the legal order, the continuous existence of the society that has that order. When the changes in the power structure, nevertheless, reach revolutionary proportions, a break in the continuum of validity sometimes seems desirable as the adequate expression for the break in the continuum of the power structure. Breaks in the continuum of the power structure, however, are phenomena within the continuum of society. Revolutionary governments often may not acknowledge this continuum, and sometimes it will require opposition in the field of foreign politics to remind a revolutionary government that a continuum of law, parallel with the continuous society, exists indeed and has not been broken by the emotionally world-destroying and world-creating events of the revolution.

IV

RULE AND NORM

We are faced with the following aporia:

On the one hand, the law is manifest phenomenally in a plurality of legal orders understood as aggregates of valid rules. These aggregates resist analysis under the categories of essence and individuation. The obstacle proves to be the validity that pervades the legal order into every single rule. When analysis pursues validity into its consequences, however, the legal order disappears from existence altogether in the Zenonic paradox. No assurances about a realm of normativity can confer ontological status on the legal order.

On the other hand, the result is at variance with the phenomena attesting the existence of "the law" in everyday parlance. In every country the statutes, the administrative orders, the administrative and judicial decisions form a literary corpus, increasing prodigiously under the legislative and administrative needs of modern industrial societies, to which no one will deny existence. "The law" exists so massively that we have professional schools, the law schools, organized for the purpose of familiarizing prospective lawyers with as much of the gigantic phenomenon as possible within the course of a few years.

The exit from the aporia opens with the recognition that the legal order, while it has no ontological status of its own, is part of the process by which a society brings itself into existence and preserves itself in ordered existence. The larger entity is the object of inquiry, and the legal order exists indeed insofar as it is part of the larger complex. We have ascertained, moreover, that the weight in the comprehensive entity lies on the social side. Assuming these results of the inquiry into the nature of the law as established, further questions now will arise concerning the manner in which the legal order and its rules participate in the existence of ordered society. The first of these questions will have to be the radical one: How is it at all possible ontologically that rules have a function in the existence of a society and its ordering process?

§ 1. The Rule and the Lastingness of Order

Again we must have recourse to the preanalytical understanding of rules or laws. When we say that something happens "as a rule," we mean that more often than not an event E will occur whenever there is a situation S. The situation S has the role of a condition for the occurrence, with a high probability, of the event E. The rule, stating the connection between S and E, expresses a strictly empirical observation. We need not assume that S is the "cause" of E, that it is desirable that E follow S, or that E "should" or "should not" occur whenever the situation S is present. All we are interested in at the moment are the ontological implications of the rule: that the situation S and the event E are recognizable, that they recur, and that they recur with a high frequency in the relation expressed by the rule. Rules, we may conclude, can have a function in society only if there are recognizable, typical situations and events, if the situations and events recur, and if they recur with such frequency in connection that the connection itself acquires the character of a recognizable type and can be expressed in "rules."

As a matter of fact, the order of a society has a discernible structure of typical elements, of typical situations and events, and of typical connections between them. Every glance at the legal order of any society will reveal the typical structure that is submitted to regulation by the rules. There are such large complexes recurring in legal orders as the civil and criminal laws. Within the civil law, for example, we find such typical subcomplexes as the law of persons, of things, of obligations, of marriage and family and of succession, covering the status of human beings, their relations to objects of the external world, their contractual relations among themselves, the order of their family units in life and death. If society were an amorphous flux, without a structure of constant elements and recurrences, rules would be of no use because they would have no field of application. Rules can be used in the ordering process because the order of society has a structure that lasts in time.

We shall speak of the "lasting" character of order so that there will be no confusion between this ontological problem and the question of general and individual norms. We speak of a general rule if the types created by the rule apply to an indefinite number of persons, actions, and situations; of an individual rule if it concerns specific persons and their actions. Whether the rule is general or individual, it can function only because the reality to which it applies is lasting. It would make no sense for A and B to contest the ownership of a piece of property if contested pieces of property had the habit of evaporating in the face of a court decision. The same is true if the organization of the life of the persons A and B would change so rapidly and radically that the question of who owns the contested piece of property would be of no interest to either A or B. The individual decision in the concrete case makes sense only under the conditions that the lives of A and B have a certain duration; that the lives have an organization with stable features; that the material conditions of, and human relations in, the lives of A and B are matters of lasting interest; and so forth. This lasting character becomes especially clear when a person A applies for restraining action to a court, as in the case of an injunction. The court is requested to enjoin another person B *not* to engage in types of action that might disturb the lasting structure of A's life or some part of it, as for instance a business enterprise; and the injunction is necessary in order to prevent the anticipated disturbance because the life of the person B also has a lasting organization that is fraught with the continued potentiality of action disturbing the life of A.

The lastingness of structure pervades the order of society into the concrete existence of every single member; and this concreteness of lasting order in the daily actions of every human being makes it necessary to have more than mere general rules for comprehensive types of situations and actions, omitting the details as "nonessential." The individual decisions in the concrete cases are necessary because the lasting order of society is essentially concrete as the order in the lives of the single members. From the side of society we are reaching again the problem of validity. We cannot divide the legal order, as we have seen, into essential and nonessential rules. Validity is of the essence of the legal order in every single rule; and this pervasive character of validity in the legal order now is revealed as expressing the pervasive concreteness in the lasting order of society.

The lasting structure of order is the structure of human existence in society. This structure is the subject matter of the *episteme politike* in the Aristotelian sense. The principal components of the lasting structure are man's organization of his physiological existence in family and household, of his utilitarian existence through division of labor and commerce, and of his intellectual and spiritual existence in political society. Here also is the realm of being—society and its order—where essentials can be distinguished from nonessentials. Nevertheless, while it is agreeable to have reached at last something that looks like firm ground, we must remember Aristotle's struggle with the problem of form and substance in society. A few reflections will clear up this point as far as it is possible.

In Aristotle's *Politics* the study of the nature of the polis (Book I) is not connected properly with the analysis of the form of the polis (Book III). The nature of human community unfolds fully in the polis because the polis provides the social environment for the full unfolding of human nature. Only a community of sufficient size and wealth will permit a division of functions to such a degree that the *bios theoretikos* is possible at least for those who desire to lead it and who are willing to undergo its labors. The polis is defined as the community in which there is room for the organization of the "good life" (Book I, and Book VII, 1–3). In Aristotle's ordinary usage of his terms, this "nature" of the polis also should be its "form."

The analysis of form in Book III, however, clashes with the ordinary, synonymous use of the terms—and this clash points to the problem that the order of a polis is not inherent in the polis in the manner in which an organismic form is inherent in the specimen of a plant or animal species; but rather, this order requires human action to make it inherent. Further, the forces that provide this action in a society may change their structure without impairing the identity of the society in which the changes occur. The organization of the lawmaking process, as we called it, and the configuration of the social forces that operate the process at a given time are not identical with the nature of order in society. Inevitably the question must be asked: If the society and its order are not identical with a given power constellation and its lawmaking process, how far must we range in the order of society to find the ultimate unit of which the power constellations of the moment are only subdivisions?

This question opens a vast field of inquiry, the details of which lie beyond the scope of our analysis. Only the outline of the problem is our concern.

Aristotle, of course, saw that the horizon of a society is larger than the power constellation of the moment. The Hellenic poleis had typical sequences of power constellations and corresponding "forms of government," running the cycle of kingship, aristocracy, popular revolt, tyrannies of the type of Peisistratus, oligarchy, and democracy of various degrees of radicalism. Not the single "form of government" but the whole sequence of forms is the minimum unit of observation for both Plato and Aristotle. The cycle of the forms of government in the polis becomes the object of inquiry. The modern cycle theories go considerably further in enlarging the horizon of society and its order. In a theory like Toynbee's, not the single Hellenic polis, the single Mesopotamian city-state, or the single modern national state is the unit of order, but the civilizational society embracing a manifold of such subunits with the whole of their historical dimension. Beyond the order of the large civilizational societies, there loom the problems of an order of all mankind—problems that become acute at various times in the history of mankind when civilizational societies clash with one another, perhaps conquer one another, so that multi-civilizational empires like the Roman without a doubt become vast units of social order. While the details are not our concern, as we said, the principle of these horizons, enlarging ultimately to the horizon of mankind, is of considerable importance for the problems of jurisprudence, as we shall see.

§ 2. The Ought in the Ontological Sense

Rules can be used for the ordering of society because the order of human existence in society has the character of lastingness. Once this first point is established, the next question is: How are rules used for the purpose of social order? In the preceding section we had to stress the nature of a rule as the observation of empirical regularities in the relations between situations, events, and actions. A legal rule, however, obviously is not meant to be a proposition that can be verified or falsified—even though the existence of a legal rule frequently will permit the prediction, with a high degree of probability, that human actions will conform to it. Legal rules are meant to be "norms," and their purpose with regard to social order is "normative." Such formulations, now, come easily in preanalytical usage, but they are fraught with thorny problems. We have noted previously, for instance, that modern codes rarely are couched in normative language and that the actual definitions and descriptions of types must be interpreted as norms, using contextual indices. The analysis, therefore, must try to isolate the normative component in the meaning of legal rules.

Rules must be used in the ordering of societies because societies are not individuals of a plant or animal species with an organismic genesis, flowering, and decay. Societies depend for their genesis, continued harmonious existence, and survival on the actions of the component human beings. The nature of man and the freedom of his action for good or bad are essential factors in the structure of society. The order of its existence is neither a mechanism nor an organism, but depends on the will of men to specify and maintain it. Moreover, the order of a society is not a blueprint to be translated, with good will, into reality. It must be discovered—with an amplitude of imagination and experimentation, of trial and error; it requires improvements and must be adapted to changing circumstances. There is the previously mentioned tension in social order between standard and achievement, between achievement and the potentiality of falling short of it, between a groping for knowledge of order and the crystallization of that knowledge in articulate rules, between the order as projected and the order as realized, between what ought to be and what is.

The ultimate, the irreducible source of this tension is a set of experiences that in an analysis of the nature of the law can be no more than adumbrated.

Man has the experience of participating, through his existence, in an order of being that embraces not only himself, but also God, the world, and society. This is the experience that can become articulate in the creation of symbols of the pervasive order of being, such as the previously indicated Egyptian *maat*, or Chinese *tao*, or Greek *nomos*. Man furthermore experiences the anxiety of the possible fall from this order of being, with the consequence of his annihilation in the partnership of being; and, correspondingly, he experiences an obligation to attune the order of his existence with the order of being. Finally, he experiences the possible fall from, and the attunement with, the order of being as dependent on his action, that is, he experiences the order of his own existence as a problem for his freedom and responsibility. Within the range of society, the realization of the order of being is experienced as the burden of man. When we refer to the "tension" in social order, we envisage this class of experiences. In order to link them more closely with the problem of "normativity" in legal rules, we can speak of them as the Ought in the ontological sense.

§ 3. The Rule as Norm

The Ought, thus, is not itself a "postulate" or a "norm" but the experienced tension between the order of being and the conduct of man. In the orbit of this tension, rules concerning social order are more than empirical observations concerning regularities of action. Since the problem of order is precisely the tension between empirical conduct and true order, legal rules, whether they are general rules or individual rules for the parties in a concrete case, have the character of projects of order. Whether or not the rule employs the formula "Thou shalt" or "Thou shalt not," it has that meaning when it projects the types to which the conduct of human beings is supposed to conform. The so-called "normativity" of the rule derives, therefore, from the ontologically real tension in the order of society.

In this normativity must be distinguished the following three components:

1. The rule, when it describes a type of action to which men "ought" to conform or, in the case of crimes, "ought not" to conform, intends to render a truth about the concrete order of the respective society. It intends to give a true answer to the question of what "ought" to be done. Under this aspect of normativity, the rule

is meant as a true proposition concerning the Ought in the ontological sense.

2. The rule, within its context of the legal order, is not merely a piece of information about the Ought of order. It has been enacted, in the course of the lawmaking process, with the intention that it be heard and obeyed by the members of the society. The normativity of the rule contains, as a second component, an appeal to those to whom it is addressed to integrate the truth about the Ought into their lives. The members of society who are defined by the rule as its addressees (*e.g.,* recipients of taxable income, landlords, corporations, insurance companies, policyholders, drivers of cars, parents, all persons in their capacities as potential thieves or murderers) are supposed to realize concretely in their conduct the order of society as envisaged by the rule.

3. Information about the truth of order and the appeal to realize it do not yet exhaust the phenomenon of normativity. A truth, in order to appeal effectively and to gain adherents, must be communicated; and an appeal will not be effective if no one listens. Hence, the rule includes, as a third component of its normativity, the claim to be heard. Ignorance of the law, as we all know, does not exculpate; a policyholder will not win a suit for an unjustified claim with the argument that he has not read the fine print. Setting aside for the moment the questions of individual court decisions and of legal transactions between private citizens, "the law" claims to be known. Its appeal is "public."

§ 4. The Public Character of the Legal Norm

The components of normativity form an inseparable unit; but especially through the third of the components, the claim to be public, a number of problems arise both in the practice of order and in legal theory. A proposition concerning a truth about order must be formulated by someone, and its appeal, to be accepted, must be directed by the proponent to the addressee. The normative meaning of a rule involves at least two persons face to face in an act of communication, even though one of the two persons may be the reflecting self that formulates a rule to be followed by the acting self.

But where is the personal proponent of the rule in the case of the law? The legal rule, especially a statutory rule under the conditions

45

of modern society, obviously is not an admonition or command issued by a dignified elder to the addressee. It is a rule created in a complicated procedure that obscures the personal contributions to its making. The procedure, furthermore, is overlaid by a symbolism that obliterates completely all personal authority, inasmuch as the laws of a modern democracy emanate from the representatives of the people in legislative assembly and ultimately from the "people" itself. No one, moreover, will indulge in the fanciful assumption that the mass of the addressees really has "heard" the law in obedience to which they supposedly order their conduct. Austin, in his analytical jurisprudence, has tried to meet the phenomenal situation with the construction that the law is the command of the sovereign. In face of the phenomena, however, the construction hardly deserves the name of "theory"; it is no more than a convenient metaphor to gloss over a problem that proved too difficult to handle.

It is a very odd phenomenal situation indeed. We may doubt that the rule's proposition concerning the Ought is particularly true; we even may suspect that some pressure group has used its influence to make the order profitable to itself and damaging to the rest of us, so that the rule in effect is deliberately untrue; we may wonder, in view of the technical defects of a law, whether anyone has made any serious effort at all to formulate a truth concerning the order of society; we may find that the rule holds little appeal to us and is not exactly convincing; we may have only the haziest notion who really made that rule—and yet we consider it a valid rule as long as, on the face of it, certain procedures were followed in its making. Moreover, we consider it addressed to us and binding for us, even though we never heard of it and are surprised greatly, when we engage in a new type of activity that has legal implications, by the rules that govern an area of social relations of which we had no previous experience. It all sounds like an elaborate game of make-believe. In fact, there is an element of the game in the situation. Plato knew it when, in his *Laws*, he spoke of the "serious play"; and a philosopher and historian of our own time, Jan Huizinga, stressed this factor in his *Homo Ludens*. But the theoretical clarification of this issue must be deferred until some other preliminaries are cleared up.

There is first of all the practical question that the game, however odd it may look, is taken seriously in every society. The legal rules really are supposed to be norms of order; and the members of the society, whatever their opinions may be, really are supposed to conduct themselves in accordance with the types of action projected by the rules. The lawmaking process indeed is ontologically part of the manner in which a society has an ordered existence; and the assumption that the rules are norms, and can be norms in relation to the addressees only if they are communicated, is considerably more than a theoretical fiction. That assumption belongs to the preanalytical sphere; and every society has elaborate arrangements in its phenomenal sphere for the purpose of achieving actual communication.

The phenomenon of which a lawyer will think immediately in this connection is the "promulgation" of the law. A law is valid only if it is made public. Some countries have special law gazettes for the publication of statutes, and their constitutions may provide that a law is in force only when a specific number of days have lapsed after publication of the respective issue of the law gazette. Our Constitution makes no specific provision for promulgation but assumes a bill to become a statute when it is approved by the president through his signature, or when ten days have lapsed after transmission of the bill to the president for his approval. Yet we have, as does every country, means of publication by which the texts of statutes are made accessible to the public quickly. We have, in addition, a *Federal Register* for the publication of administrative orders, and a wealth of other means for the publication of court decisions, decisions of administrative agencies, decisions and opinions of the attorney general, and so forth.

Even this enormous apparatus, nevertheless, will not sound very convincing to the ordinary citizen who never in his life will look at any of these publications. He will object that, in spite all this effort, only the lawyers know about the law—and his observation may be tinged with the flavor of complaint about a racket. While the complaint may draw for its flavor on personal experiences, the objection definitely is unjustified. For it is precisely the function of the lawyer to fill the gap between the publication machinery, both of the government and of private publishing companies, and the knowledge of the lay member of society.

To know the law requires a professional dedication that absorbs the whole man. The citizen whose time and energy are absorbed by the work in which he has specialized cannot be a legal expert at the same time—hardly under primitive social and economic conditions and certainly not under the conditions of contemporary society. The layman, when a complicated legal question arises in the course of his daily business, must supplement his fragmentary knowledge of the law with a lawyer's expert knowledge. The lawyer's knowledge is *his* knowledge of the law. Hence, when a man engages in some complicated business without legal advice and comes to grief, we shall not pity him as the victim of the unjustified assumption that the addressee of the law knows the law, but shall rather berate him for his imprudence if not stupidity.

The legal profession as an estate in society, thus, has a public function in maintaining the order of society insofar as the lawyer's professional knowledge is the mediator between the legal order and the citizen's knowledge of the law. This state of things is recognized phenomenally through the institutional provision for the training of lawyers, for the maintenance of standards, for rules of professional ethics, for appropriate counsel for defendants in criminal cases, and through the private organization of legal aid for persons who cannot afford lawyers.

In the light of these observations on promulgation and the lawyer's function, the assumption that the citizen knows the law, and by virtue of his knowledge is bound by it, will look somewhat less fantastic. But precisely this elaborate social installation for communicating knowledge of the law makes it even clearer that the normativity of the legal rule is not merely one person's command to another person.

V

THE RULE AS PROJECT

We had to place the rules of the legal order, with their peculiar normativity, in the context of the lawmaking process. In its turn, we had to place the lawmaking process in the larger context of a society to whose members the norms are addressed. The norms, thus, acquired the character of projects for the concrete order of society;

and at the core of this order we found the Ought in the ontological sense, the tension in society that requires the elaborate efforts to create and maintain the order and, with the order, the very existence of society.

If now we position ourselves at the ontological center of the tension, we see that the lawmaking process is only one among several types of efforts to project and realize the order of society. This is not surprising, for the social order is not the lawmakers' business alone but also that of every member of the society. The organization of a man's personal life with regard to his work, the maintenance of himself and his family, the calculability of the future for which he must lay plans, the prospects of his success in business, the nature of business that he can undertake in view of the stability or instability of order, the possibilities of social rise, the prospects for the future of his children, and so forth, are interwoven inextricably with the social order as a whole.

Human existence is social, and there is no clear line that would separate personal from social order. Every society is buzzing with debate about the justice and injustice, the advantage and disadvantage of the order as it exists, and this debate issues in reflections about the law: what the law ought to be or ought not to be, what old laws are no longer suitable to present conditions, what other laws should be made, what abuses occur under the present law, what should be done about it, etc. The whole society is alive with projects of order in various degrees of articulation and rationality, of reforming goodwill and violent resentment, of effective pressure and impotent rage. A brief glance at these phenomena will be of assistance in distinguishing more clearly the specific normativity of the projects called "the law."

§ 1. The Two Types of Projects

Two classes of phenomena are of interest for our purpose: 1) projects intended to be realized empirically in a concrete society, and 2) projects intended to set standards of true order, but with little or no expectation of their being realized concretely.

In the first class belong a variety of phenomena that can be arranged in the order of their distance from the lawmaking process in the technical sense. Closest to that process, and blending into it, are the preparations for the enactment of a statute. Under the Constitution, the legislative process begins with the introduction of a bill by a member of Congress in his respective house. The legally relevant act of introduction, therefore, is set in an environment of projective efforts by persons who have an interest in a bill of that content becoming law. Such a person may be the representative acting on his own initiative or, more frequently, at the request of constituents or other interested individuals and groups, with the help of independent lawyers or of the legislative drafting service. Strange things may happen to a bill after its introduction, when a committee gets to work on it, amends it in various ways, combines it with other bills concerning the same subject, and finally reports to the House a bill that perhaps nobody has ever introduced.

In all countries the executive branch of the government has a special function in the preparation of bills. In countries with parliamentary constitutions, the members of the cabinet can introduce bills, and these bills are prepared by the bureaucracy. Under our Constitution, while the executive branch has no right to introduce bills, it introduces bills *de facto* through influential members of Congress. In either case, such bills are not prepared in a vacuum but articulate legislative projects that reflect the wishes of various groups in the community, either directly or in the circuitous fashion of campaign promises on the basis of which the government in power has been elected; and inevitably the policies of influential bureaucrats will be an additional factor to be reckoned with in the formulation of the project.

Beyond this area of immediate preparation for the lawmaking process lies the much vaster area of the debate *de lege ferenda*. Here we find the discussion of desirable legislation by various associations and institutions, with its ramifications in the press, in periodicals, in memoranda, together with the multitude of means by which pressure groups bring their wishes before the public. A very important subphenomenon in this class, covering a large area of social order, is the drafting of model codes by various professional associations and institutions created for that purpose. In all these cases we can speak of projects for projects, or projects in the second degree.

Still further removed from the immediate projects, and still vaster in extent, is the general political debate concerning social reforms in the light of principles that, if ever coming closer to realization, will require implementation by a huge body of new legislation. If, for example, in a society that hitherto has had no institutions of these kinds, a political party makes it its program to introduce free medical service for everyone, or to nationalize large segments of the country's industry, as occurred not long ago in Great Britain, elaborate efforts extending over many years are necessary, not only to convert public opinion to programs of this type, but also to prepare the drafts of the implementing bills in concrete detail.

By the phenomena of this variety we are referred further back into the political process, the formation of political parties and their programs, the articulation and adaptation of policies for the purpose of vote-getting, etc. Beyond this area of the political process at large lies a fringe of the more or less unsuccessful voicing of opinions about desirable reforms of order, ranging from the reasonable but unpopular to the unreasonably Utopian and downright pathological.

The project character of the rules, thus, unfolds an amplitude of phenomena that includes, at one end, the plain and sober suggestion to amend a law that has proved unsatisfactory in practice and, at the other end, the Utopian's projects for world-federation and perpetual peace.

The project phenomena of the first class, however distant from the lawmaking process itself and however remote from any possibility of realization, are at least by their intention projects to be translated into the reality of social order. Considerably more intricate are the phenomena of the second class, represented by the model constitutions as we find them in the classic philosophers, Plato and Aristotle. To be sure, such models also have the character of projects; and that character even is stressed, as for instance in Plato's *Laws*, when the model arises from a dialogue with the member of a commission that is charged with the draft of a constitutional project for a colony about to be founded. It is flat nonsense, nevertheless, to interpret such models, as contemporary authors so frequently do, as Utopias, as ideal constitutions (whatever that means) that reveal the impractical or unrealistic mind of the typical philosopher. Plato and Aristotle were astute observers of the surrounding political scene, considerably more realistic than the ruling politicians and the people, who did not see the handwriting on the wall and who could not resolve on appropriate measures until the Macedonian conquest put an end to their petty quarrels. The philosophers not only understood the nature of the Macedonian threat to the existence of the polis but also were quite aware—and more than once said so expressly—that the polis was rotten beyond hope and ready for the fall. In that situation, as they fully understood, projects for the reform of the order of the polis would have been worse than "unrealistic"—they would have been silly. If Plato and Aristotle undertook the labors of constructing their models while the polis was approaching disaster before their eyes—and actually was overcome by it ten years after Plato's death and during the life of Aristotle—their work was not a project for the improvement of an obviously dead order. In search of their motives one need not indulge in fantastic speculations but may accept their word for it that they were engaged in an inquiry concerning the truth about order in society—an inquiry, to be sure, motivated by the absence of true order in the surrounding society, but an inquiry that will have its validity as a work of the *episteme politike* even if the society that inspired it was moribund and could no longer be saved by the medicine.

The inquiry into the true order of society, regardless of the question whether the surrounding society is a suitable field for its realization, develops, in the classic philosophers, into an autonomous occupation of the human mind—an enterprise that can be successful only because the true order of society is the order in which man can unfold fully the potentialities of his nature. The nature of man, his Logos, becomes the central theme of a science of social order; the science of human nature, philosophical anthropology, becomes the centerpiece of political science; and the nature of man, as it unfolds in the existence of the philosopher, as well as in the disordered human existence of the surrounding society, becomes the empirical material for the inquiry. The true order of society is living reality in the well-ordered soul of the philosopher, brought to sharp consciousness by the philosopher's refusal to succumb to the disorder of his environment.

§ 2. The Empirical and the Philosophical Lawmaking Processes

At the moment we are concerned, not with the results of the Platonic-Aristotelian work, but with its intention. The philosophers develop projects of order that they do not expect to be enacted as valid rules through the lawmaking process of their society. The work is done when the dialogue or treatise is written; the projection of the true order is finished. If conditions should arise historically under which such an order could be enacted by an empirical society, all the better, though neither Plato nor Aristotle expects to see these conditions fulfilled. The philosopher, thus, becomes the lawmaker of the true order in his own right, rivaling the lawmaker of the empirical society with its order of dubious truth. This lawmaking on two levels, as it arises phenomenally in the history of mankind, specifically in the Hellas of the fourth century, brings into focus the tension between the empirical society, with its empirical order made in its empirical lawmaking process, and the true order of society that originates in the Ought in the ontological sense as experienced by the philosopher. The problem of the law is not exhausted by the mere existence of a society under any kind of order that happens to be created by the lawmaking process. The empirical law can be measured by the standards of the true law developed by the philosopher.

The two lawmaking processes, the empirical and the philosophical, are related to one another. The philosophical analysis penetrates to the essence of the Ought in the ontological sense; and on the basis of the insights gained, the philosopher tries to sketch the types of conduct that would be adequate optimally to translate the truth about order, as it lives in the soul of the philosopher, into the practice of society. The weight of the work lies, therefore, in the inquiry into the nature of true order. The model projects, while more than literary devices, have the character of secondary elaborations and must not be taken as rules with autonomous validity. A glance at Plato's *Laws* shows that the "laws" play quantitatively a rather insignificant role in comparison with the preambles, *i.e.*, with the lengthy exposition of the reasons for their formulation. Modern interpreters frequently have complained that Plato's project of law in the *Republic* is fragmentary, omitting whole areas of law from consideration—a complaint to which Plato himself gave the answer that anyone can elaborate the legal projects if he has understood the essence of order and realized the order within his own life. Aristotle conducts his analysis of the essence of order through ten books of *Ethics* and six books of *Politics* before, in *Politics* VII and the fragmentary VIII, he turns to the elaboration of his model.

Yet, though the models are secondary to the analysis of essence, they are not superfluous. The philosopher's analysis is motivated by the resistance of substantive order in himself to the disorder in empirical society. The philosopher's work is an act of judgment on the empirical order, animated by the claim that the empirical order should conform more closely to types that will express adequately the truth of order. The philosopher is not outside the sphere of law-making, even if he knows that the empirical society will not heed his advice. On the contrary, since the Ought in the ontological sense is the reality of order, the empirical lawmaking process has moved too far from reality to have the full weight of normativity. The philosopher, therefore, while not starting a revolution in his country (an escape expressly rejected by Plato), will withdraw from participation in the lawmaking process and refuse office lest he become an accomplice in the unjust actions of the government. The responsibility of lawmaking devolves on him when the makers of the empirical law become derelict in their duties. The philosopher's models, thus, are connected intimately with the empirical order as the standards of its normativity.

The philosopher's project and the empirical order, moreover, are not flatly opposed, but linked by transitional projects approaching more or less closely the reality of the Ought. Hence, Plato not only has developed the project of the polis in which the philosophers are kings, but has envisaged, in the *Laws*, a second-best polis. In this polis, the rulers, though not philosophers themselves, are trained in the results of philosophy as a creed so that in the light of a philosophical minimum dogma they will make the laws as best they can. Plato even contemplated the possibility of third- and fourth-best projects, if the second- or third-best also should prove too hard for the weakness of man to bear under the empirical circumstances.

Our concern here is not, however, the detail of Plato's far-flung work but its principle: the empirical order of a society is capable of degrees of reality in the measure in which it articulates the tension of the Ought in the ontological sense that is the object of philosophical inquiry. The normativity of the law is participation in the true order. It is a substantive normativity, not a formal one. Not just anything that is made the content of the legal order is law beyond further questioning. If the substantive normativity of the law-making process sinks too low, there will be dissatisfaction in the society that can assume revolutionary proportions—unless the situation has degenerated to a point beyond repair and the substantive dissolution of the society makes it a prey to conquest. This has become an eminently practical problem in our time, when the rise of ideological dictatorships, with their brutal suppression of true order in the life of man, acutely raises the question of how the conflict between true order and the massive power of an empirical order lacking in normative substance will end.

VI
THE IMPERSONAL VALIDITY OF LEGAL RULES

The analysis now can return to the question that motivated the survey of the project phenomena, *i.e.*, to the peculiar normativity of legal rules. Rules, we said, are addressed by one person to another person; they intend to express a truth about order; they appeal to the addressee to conform his conduct to the normative truth of the rule; and, in order to have their effect, they must be communicated. In all of these respects the legal rules proved to be peculiar. It is difficult to ascertain the person who issues them; their truth frequently is questionable; their appeal may not be very successful; and the communication leaves much to be desired. The phenomena of law just surveyed now can be introduced into the analysis.

§ 1. Society as a Self-Organizing Entity

Rules intend to convey a truth about order. They refer ultimately to the Ought in the ontological sense, that is, to the experienced tension between the order of being and that part of the order that has to be established in society through human action. At the on-

55

tological core of normativity we find two persons who issue rules to acting man: 1) God, and 2) reflecting man, using his reason and conscience. Beyond this ontological core expands the existence of man in society; and within this realm of social existence other persons may address norms to him—parents, friends, teachers, elders, priests, philosophers, and government officials. For all of these cases of rules that emanate from other persons within the concrete society, the analysis must proceed with utmost caution and discipline, because the slightest concession to conventional beliefs will lead to wildly erroneous constructions. We must insist, in apparent conflict with all preanalytical language, that beyond the two persons of the ontological core there is no one who can issue rules with normative authority. There is a *ius divinum et naturale*, but there is definitely no autonomous *ius sociale et historiale*. All rules directed from person to person within a society must rely for their normative authority on the ontological core.

Only when this point is established and held firmly will the problem presented by rules that demand obedience by virtue of their social authority come into view at all. We already have rejected Austin's construction of the law as the command of the sovereign as a superficial metaphor that does not even touch the problem; and we may add that, for the same reason, we must reject the command theories developed later in the nineteenth century, especially by German scholars. This problem will have to be unfolded analytically from the preanalytical observation that the making and issuing of social rules, as we shall call the genus of which the legal rules are a species, is a process within society itself.

The implications of this simple observation are very difficult to pursue because the analysis is obstructed by everyday language more concerned with tensions within the social field than with the unity of the field that is fissured by the tension. We are accustomed to speak in the dichotomies of ruler and subject, government and people, parents and children, commanders and soldiers, and so forth, and are apt to forget the embracing entity of the society *within* which the respective relations of command and obedience occur. Human existence is ontologically social, all conflicts between man and the impersonal force of the social field, of which he exists as a part, notwithstanding. Existence in society, by force of birth and nurture within a family, is ontologically, not by choice, the manner of human existence. The alternative to existence in one concrete society—short of not being born at all or of committing suicide—is not solitary existence but existence in another concrete society. The organization of man's personal life in attunement with the truth of order is possible only within the framework of social order. A society has a *raison d'être*, therefore, only insofar as it allows its members to order their lives in truth.

The various aspects of this problem have been seen in theoretical constructions of the meaning of government and society. Aristotle insisted that a society was ordered truly only when it made possible the *bios theoretikos*. Our American official creed insists that government is an organization for the purpose of securing life, liberty, and the pursuit of happiness to the people who live under it— though our creed is somewhat less clear than Aristotle on the nature of happiness. Rousseau insisted strongly on the identity of ruler and ruled in the making of the law, so that the social rules are made by those who obey them. In this identification of ruler and ruled, he could build on the earlier construction of Hobbes that man, as a member of society, abolishes his personality and receives the order of his life back through the order emanating from the sovereign he has created.

One could enlarge the observations both on phenomena and constructions, but no enlargement will add to the analytical result: society is a self-organizing entity; its rules are issued neither from a society outside its members to its members nor from a person outside society to society; society exists inasmuch as it develops a self-ordering process, and the self-ordering process is the manner of its existence. Society, one might say, issues the social rules, including the legal rules, to itself. That formulation, to be sure, is nonsense, because a rule is what a person issues to another person. But precisely this nonsense formula will sharpen the awareness for the difficulty in the analysis of the legal order, that is, the impersonal character of the legal rule.

The legal rule has neither a personal addresser nor a personal addressee. This difficulty cannot be overcome by erecting society, the state, or the sovereign into a fictitious personal addresser and by erecting the common man, who is only vaguely familiar with the law, into the fictitious addressee who hears the rules addressed to him. For this reason, we had to reject the command theories that indulge in these constructions. For the same reason we must reject the attempts to arrive at a "definition" of the legal rule by first forming a genus "rule," and then distinguishing specifically between autonomous and heteronomous rules, or by making sanction by governmentally organized force the specific difference that distinguishes legal rules from the rules of customs and mores enforced by social pressure and from moral rules enforced by conscience or fear of God. Such distinctions by textbook logic move on the preanalytical level. The classification of phenomena is of no use when an ontological problem requires analysis.

§ 2. The Representation of Society

Legal rules are impersonal insofar as they are not issued by a person. Since only persons can issue rules it would seem to follow that legal rules cannot exist at all and that what commonly goes under this name does not have the character of a rule but is something entirely different. That conclusion, however, would be at variance with our everyday experience and parlance about legal rules. Since, on the one hand, the analytical result will have to stand, and since, on the other hand, the analysis, as we have stressed repeatedly, must not make nonsense of the preanalytical experience, we must return to the phenomena for supplementary indications of the nature of the law. The problem that suggests itself most urgently is created by the question: How can a society, not being a person, issue rules at all?

The answer to this question is plain on the phenomenal level: since society, a non-person, cannot issue rules, utterances in the form of rules that emanate from real persons are considered, under certain conditions, to be valid rules for the conduct of members of the society. Obviously, not every such utterance emanating from persons at random is accorded the character of validity. When a person with convictions stronger than his intelligence takes it upon himself to lecture us upon what we ought to do, we ignore his advice; and when he persists, and his harangues take up too much of our time, we tell him to mind his own business. The would-be lawmaker is a common figure in every society, and we can distinguish him from the real lawmaker, to whom we accord status as the representative of society. A multitude of men exists as an ordered society inasmuch as it is articulated into rulers and ruled. A society comes into existence through social articulation that results in the creation and acceptance of a representative, and it remains in existence as long as it has accepted representatives. Organization for action, both internal and external, through a representative, is the manner in which a society exists. The lawmaking process, from the making of the constitution to the individual administrative and judicial decisions, is the self-organization of society for its ordered existence through representatives.

The genesis of society through creation and acceptance of a representative, and the vicissitudes of representation in a society after it has come into existence, form a vast field of study in political science. It lies beyond the scope of the present analysis. We are concerned with representation only as an essential factor in the lawmaking process. The legal rules indeed are made by human beings, not by their authority as persons, but by authority of their status as representatives of society. Since the lawmaker acts as a representative, not as a person, it is possible to create collective organs of lawmaking, such as legislative assemblies, whose acts clearly have impersonal, representative character. The distinction between person and representative holds true also in the cases of rules emanating from a single human being, as for instance from a single judge holding court. We accept the decision of the single judge sitting in court as valid, not because of the wisdom and justice of his decision, but because he is the representative of society whose position derives ultimately from the constitution. We abide by his decision, not because we agree with its truth—probably we shall hold a different opinion about the truth when the decision has gone against us—but because we play, in our capacity as citizens, our representative roles as members of the organized society who respect its order.

§ 3. The Calculus of Error

This play of representation is performed, not as *l'art pour l'art*, but as a necessity for the ordered existence of man in society. Its purpose is the realization of order; and order is not somebody's pleas-

59

ure but the substantive organization of human life in attunement with the order of being as it is experienced in the Ought in the ontological sense.

Since the representative, whether higher or lower in the hierarchy of the lawmaking process, whether collective or individual, is human in every sense of the word, he may abuse his representative position and issue rules that depart widely from the truth of order. These phenomena of abuse are constant ingredients in the practice of every social order; they have attracted the theorist's attention from the very beginnings of the *episteme politike* and have motivated attempts at theoretical construction. Plato and Aristotle already distinguish between good and bad forms of government according to whether the representative of the moment pursues the common good or some private good. The government of the one, the few, or the many is good if the representative pursues the common good; it is bad if the representative pursues his private interests. The three good forms are called monarchy, aristocracy, and polity respectively; the three bad forms are called tyranny, oligarchy, and democracy. Again we are concerned at this point, not with the content that can be given to the concept of the common good, but with the phenomenon of its formation for the purpose of establishing the link between the lawmaking process and the ontological substance of order.

The tension between the substance of order and the possible abuse of the lawmaking process, moreover, is not merely an object of contemplation for the philosopher but the motive for more or less elaborate experiments with institutional safeguards against its potential abuse. The separation of powers, the Bill of Rights, the independent judiciary, universal suffrage, and the election of the representatives for relatively short terms of office are, under our Constitution, the devices for reducing the possibility of abuse to a minimum. But even the best devices are not foolproof and do not work under all circumstances, for the institutional checks on the representative must themselves be staffed by human beings who are not beyond the weaknesses of man. In particular, the devices of universal suffrage and frequent elections have proved disappointing in many cases because the assumption that the mass of common men is the mysterious repository of the will to substantive order is wrong. The common man, to be sure, is the principal sufferer when the government is bad, and the voice of the people usually is right when it is raised in complaint. But from such true observations it does not follow that governments elected and approved enthusiastically by the majority of the people are particularly good—as recent instances of totalitarian governments have shown.

The tension between true order and empirical order, we conclude, never can be abolished, though the discrepancy can be held, by various devices, to a minimum that will not motivate the people to revolt. Even a not-so-good representative may be preferable to a violent upheaval, given the inevitable and incalculable disorganization of life that accompanies a revolution and the not-at-all-certain prospect that the next representative will be any better than his predecessor. The undisturbed order of the society enters as a good in its own right into the normativity of the legal rules. In every society, the lawmaking process rests for its validity on the understanding that a considerable margin of error must be allowed with regard to the truth of order in the ontological sense. Although there are limits to the proportions that the error may assume, existence in an imperfectly ordered society, with numerous and even gross injustices in single cases, is preferable to disorder and violence. The calculus of error included in the lawmaking process through representatives of society is a further component in the impersonal character of the positive law. The legal rule is neither a personal rule of reason and conscience nor a rule of divine law in the Decalogue or the Sermon on the Mount.

§ 4. The Use of Force

We must consider, finally, the element in the validity of the legal rule that many theorists are inclined, without further analysis, to make its specific characteristic, *i.e.*, its sanction through force.

The use of force for the imposition of the legal order is necessary for a number of reasons. The first of these reasons is the just-discussed calculus of error. Since there is a discrepancy between true order and empirical order, enforcement is necessary in order to eliminate disobedience on the part of citizens contending that the content of the rule is not in accord with the Ought in the ontological sense. We do not have to adduce extreme cases for illustration. We only have to imagine what would happen if taxpayers could refuse payment until the expenditures of the government stand rational scrutiny in the light of true order. The Rivers and Harbors Bill alone would provide sufficient reason to refuse the payment of taxes. The debate about the justice of the law must remain within the forms of political criticism and political action through voting. If the existence of the society is to be preserved, the debate cannot be permitted to degenerate into individual decision and resistance.

Force is necessary, second, because the question of truth in matters of order rarely permits a certain, unequivocal answer. The structure of a society, especially of a modern industrial society, is infinitely complex; which of the various possible policies concerning a specific problem is in agreement with the common good, and therefore should be implemented by law, will be a matter of pros and cons with no clear weight on one side or the other. The decision, when finally made, will contain an element of arbitrariness. Again, if the society is to survive, the debate cannot go on forever; and once the decision is made by the representative, disobedience on the ground that the merits of the measure are still open to doubt cannot be permitted.

The third and final reason why the sanction by force is necessary is the one to which Aristotle accords prime importance. The whole social organization for making and enforcing the law would be superfluous, he argues, if men would act in accordance with true order without compulsion or the threat of compulsion. If men were motivated always by the *aidos*, piety or shame, to refrain from doing what is wrong and shameful, what defiles their stature as men; or if, in the case of possible lapse, admonitions by fellowmen would be sufficient to make the potential wrongdoer aware of what he is doing and shame him into right conduct; then there would be no need for the law and its enforcement as the organization of society for maintaining its order.

But that is not the nature of man. To be sure, it is the nature of man to be a person, that is, to order his conduct by reason and conscience. But it is also the nature of man not to be a person. In the first place, man does not spring into the world as a full-grown person but is born as a child. His personality is a structure in the soul that grows slowly and hardly achieves maturity before the age of thirty. With some it takes longer. A large proportion of men never reach full personal stature, and sometimes their growth stops very early. For the full-grown man, Aristotle uses the term *spoudaios*, the mature man—but when he speaks about the possibility of realizing a true order in the Hellenic polis, he remarks that probably in no Greek polis could be found even one hundred mature men who could form the nucleus of an adequate ruling group. Besides the children who lack the full development of personality, there are in every society "slaves by nature," that is, men who, for one reason or another, never grow to maturity but need social pressures, energetic reminders, and ultimately the threat of force to keep them on the straight path. They still may be useful members of society by virtue of their special skills; but they are not the members who can let the substance of order that lives in man flow into the order of society and thereby sustain it, for too little of that substance lives in them. Contemporary social scientists have observed the same human types as Aristotle and speak of them as the inward-directed and outward-directed personalities—language that may become ontologically misleading, since the point is precisely that the outward-directed personalities are so directed because they are deficient in personality.

Obviously, we can distinguish a wide variety of human types on the scale of maturity and immaturity, ranging from the saint and philosopher to the habitual criminal. Such types in fact have become the object of extensive studies. What is important for the present analysis, however, is not the empirical study of the types, but the fact that this amplitude of types has its roots in the nature of man. Those forces in the soul that disturb the attunement of the person with the order of being are as essentially human as the experience of order and the desire for attunement. Every man has to carry the burden of his all-too-human passions—of his pride and inertia, his aggressiveness and lack of courage, his righteous indignation and lack of wisdom, his dullness and lack of imagination, his complacency and indifference, his ignorance and folly. In brief: the nature of man is not all personal. On the contrary, it contains a powerful sector of urges, passions, concupiscences that not only are impersonal but even obstruct the formation and action of the personal center in the soul. Hence, the use of force in society is not necessary for imposing a true order on the person of man—that matter would take care of itself if man were all person. It is necessary for imposing an order bearing the marks of human personality on the impersonal nature of man. In particular, the use of force is necessary to break the impersonality of man when it tends to disrupt the order of human existence in society.

With regard to this last point, however, some caution is suggested. The order of human existence in society, as well as the use of force, must be understood in the fullness of its ontological meaning. Perhaps the use of force is not primarily a means "to protect society" against the lawbreaker. While punishment, for example, certainly has the function of protecting the members of a society against the disorganization of their lives by the disturbing actions of their fellow members, it also has the purpose of restoring the personal order in the soul of the delinquent and, as far as that is possible, of reconstructing him as a person. A utilitarian "philosophy" of criminal law would obscure the problem that, in the order and disorder of society, the Ought in the ontological sense is at stake and that this Ought has its seat in the person of every single man.

The use of force in the imposition of the legal order, we may summarize, brings to ultimate clarity the impersonal nature of the legal rule: the impersonality of the legal order has its ontological source in the impersonality of human nature.

VII
CONCLUSIONS

We started the analysis from the everyday experience of the law and penetrated from its phenomenal surface to its ontological core. We now can summarize the results of the analysis.

§ 1. The Components of Validity

The legal order has no ontological status of its own. As long as it is the object of study without relation to its context, the validity of its rules is nothing but the timeless meaning of propositions. The constructions applied to this body of meanings lead into the impasse of the Zenonic paradox. With the introduction of contextual phenomena, however, the validity of the rules acquires a body of reality. We now can list the components of this validity as the first result of the analysis:

1. Legal rules, to begin with, are propositions concerning the order of human existence in society. We had to qualify this structure of their meaning, however, by the observation that the actual content of a law frequently does not use a normative formula. The text of a law, more often than not, offers descriptions and definitions concerning situations of fact, events, and human actions. Although the intended meaning of the descriptions and definitions can be rounded out without difficulty by supplying the normative formula, it is important to note that the lawmaker relies on contextual phenomena, that is, on interpretations by members of the society, to articulate the full meaning of his work. The very structure of meaning points beyond the rule toward the field of social reality in which the legal order gains its peculiar validity.

2. A legal rule is not a meaning in a vacuum. It is part of a society in ordered existence. It is integrated into the reality of the society by making the conduct of members of the society its contents. It does not refer to human conduct, however, with the intent of advancing a true proposition, based on empirical observation, about the behavior of human beings. A legal rule is not a proposition in science. Its intention is not cognitive. This is so even though, in a well-functioning society, allowing for a margin of failure, the conduct of men in certain situations can be predicted if one knows what the law is, for their conduct generally is oriented toward the legal rules. It is this predictability that motivates erroneous constructions concerning the nature of the law.

3. While the intention of the rule is not cognitive, the rule nevertheless intends a truth. That is the point perhaps most difficult to understand in the contemporary state of philosophical disintegration. Normativity is not a quality that attaches to the grammatical form of the imperative or to the normative formulas "Thou shalt" and "Thou shalt not." We are not obliged to do something just because somebody tells us "Do this" or "Do that," not even if it should prove the better part of prudence to obey because he points a revolver at us. In order to bring out its complete meaning, we always must translate the language of normativity into the fuller "It is true that you should do this or that." The truth of the resulting

proposition is subject to examination, just as is the truth of a proposition with cognitive intention concerning events in the world of sense experiences.

The examination, which must be conducted in the light of Reason and Revelation, is in the nature of the case considerably more difficult than the examination of a truth concerning sense data. Still, the Ought is a reality in the experiences we have outlined. One always can conduct the argument within the general form: if this is the nature of man, and if it is the purpose of human existence to bring this nature to its full realization as far as it is possible within the limitations of human powers, then this course of action is preferable to another course. The normative character of an action contemplated by the rule does not attach to the form of the rule, as we said, but to the action envisaged; and whether or not the alleged character of normativity attaches really to the type of action is a question subject to critical examination. Any other construction would abandon the ontological tension of the Ought and put the question of order at the mercy of force. The validity of the legal rule, thus, contains the component of normativity in the ontological sense.

4. Obviously, however, the validity of the legal rule contains more than the normativity of the ontological Ought. The *ius positivum* is not the *ius divinum et naturale*. Into the validity of the legal rule there enters as a further component the impersonal existence of man in society. Because of the function of the representative, the calculus of error, and sanction by force, this impersonal factor pervades the lawmaking process from its inception in the creation of the representative to the enforcement of individual decisions in concrete cases. This authority of power, as we may call it, is not an additional source of normativity, for there is no existence of man independent of the order of society. The order of human existence is indivisibly the order of human existence in society. And the Ought, as it discloses itself in the experience of tension between empirical and true order, embraces the discipline of passion both individual and social. There *ought* to be, human nature being what it is, an organization of society with the power of making and enforcing the law, for society is, in the constitution of being, ineluctably the way of human existence. While the power of the representative and his lawmaking function is not an

independent source of normativity, it is a separate source of the validity of the legal rule, by the side of the two normative sources of reason and revelation.

§ 2. The Legal Order and the Historically Concrete Society

In listing the components of validity, we had to touch incidentally on a number of points that we now must formulate explicitly as further results of the analysis:

1. While the legal order and its validity are rooted in the nature of man and his existence in society, the content of the legal order cannot be deduced from the nature of man. Between human existence in society and the representative's effort to order it by means of the lawmaking process, there is interposed the existence of society in historical concreteness. Societies not only are not mechanisms or organisms as far as the functioning of their "form" is concerned, they are not even replicas of one another with regard to their organized "form." There are small and large societies; there are nomadic, agricultural, commercial, and industrial societies; there are tribal communities, city states, nation states, and empires. There are societies that live in the form of cosmological myth, and others that have differentiated the orders of revelation and reason.

The enumeration of phenomenal types at this point intends no more than to suggest the great problem that society itself is not merely a specimen of a species but includes in its nature the historical unfolding of true order. That problem has been seen by the classic philosophers. Both Plato and Aristotle know that the site and size of the territory, the number of citizens, the type of economy and state of technology, the civilizational and educational state of the people are all relevant for the realization of a true order that will articulate optimally the Ought in the ontological sense. In a very small community, under cramped economic conditions, with little relation with the outside world, and no appreciable means for personal education and development, even the best order possible under such conditions will give little opportunity for unfolding the potentialities of human nature. Hence, the questions of the legal order are far from exhausted by the assurance that the personal and impersonal elements of human nature are components of its validity. There are the further questions of the optimal order under the given historical conditions and of the legal technique for achieving the best possible results. From the side of the historical concreteness of society arises again the problem that we encountered from the side of validity: the order of society is concrete throughout, and correspondingly the legal order is valid throughout.

2. There is a corollary result that in this context we can indicate only briefly. Since the law has its function in the concrete ordering of society, there is no history of the law in the strict sense. History enters the law from the side of society. Since the order of man in society has a history, and since the law is concerned with the regulation of human conduct under concrete conditions, the institutions of the law have a history indirectly through their participation in the history of human existence in society.

3. For an inquiry into the nature of the law, the most important event in the history of social order is the differentiation of the normative sources of authority, of reason and revelation, from the compact experiences and symbols of the myth. Under this aspect we must distinguish between three principal types of law: a) the law in the context of a society that is ordered by the cosmological myth; b) the law in the contexts of societies that have experienced Revelation (Israel) or Philosophy (late Hellenic, classical Roman); and c) the law in the contexts of the Roman Empire and Western civilization, in which both reason and revelation are present as authoritative sources of order. Today this problem is neglected badly in jurisprudence—one might even say it is completely disregarded—because our cultural environment has become both antireligious and antiphilosophical.

Nevertheless, the relation of the three authorities of Power, Reason, and Revelation obviously is of the first importance for the realization of true order in society, once the normative authorities have been differentiated from the myth. One may formulate tentatively that the balance of the three authorities is the condition of true order in Western civilization. That question has acquired a new pungency in the nineteenth and twentieth centuries, both practical and theoretical, because of the rise of Gnostic creed movements that attempt the ordering of society by fusing the normative authority into the authority of power, as it is done for instance in the organization of a Communist or National Socialist empire. That fusion of the authorities would have to be added as a fourth type to the three just enumerated, for deliberate fusion of differentiated components is not the same as primordial compactness. The distinction of the great historical types of order, in the context of which the lawmaking processes function, must be considered a further, and the final, result of this inquiry into the nature of the law.

2

Outline of Jurisprudence Course

LAW 112, LOUISIANA STATE UNIVERSITY
LAW SCHOOL
1954–1957

Jurisprudence

I. Delimitation of the Field
1. The historical character of the concepts used in delimitation
2. The three balancing forces of high civilizations: State, Church, Philosophy
3. The penetration of legal order with reason
4. The role of science at the various levels of law making
5. Classification of legal theories according to the position assumed by the theorist in the process of law making

II. The Origins of Jurisprudence
1. Justinian's enactment of jurisprudence as law
2. The definitions of justice and jurisprudence
3. The definitions of natural, civil, and gentic law [ius gentium]
4. The jurisprudent as lawmaker, statesman, philosopher, and priest
5. The component elements of Justinian's jurisprudence

III. The Primary Experiences of Social Order
1. Social order through participation in cosmic order (China, Babylon, Egypt)
2. Social order through participation in the revealed will of God (Israel)
3. Social order through participation of the psyche in the divine logos (Hellenic philosophers)
4. Social order through participation in the spirit of Christ (the corpus mysticum)

IV. The Succession of Legal Cultures in the West
1. The Ancient Near Eastern (Babylonian, Hittite, and Israelite Codes)
2. The Roman (Republic, Principate, Dominate, Justinian)
3. The Western (Roman Vulgar Law, Germanic Tribal Law, Canon Law, Revival of Roman Law, the English development)

V. Social Crisis and Reflection on the Meaning of Law
1. The crisis of Israel and the Prophets
2. The Mycenaean catastrophe and the early Greek thinkers on law (from Hesiod to Heraclitus)
3. The disintegration of [the polis in] the fifth century and the Sophistic philosophy of law
4. The philosophic opposition of Socrates-Plato
5. Aristotle
6. The Hellenistic and Roman empires and the Stoic philosophy of law (from Zeno to Marcus Aurelius)
7. The Roman crisis and the imperial response—Justinian
8. The Roman crisis and the Christian response—Saint Augustine
9. The crisis of the high Middle Ages and Saint Thomas

VI. The Secular National State
1. The medieval conception of the Monarchia—Dante
2. Legal and political sovereignty of the closed national state—Bodin
3. Spiritual sovereignty of the national state—Hobbes
4. Economic sovereignty of the national state—Fichte

5. The new philosophy of international and natural law in the fifteenth and sixteenth centuries (from Vitoria to Locke)

VII. The Theory of Positive Law
    1. Austinian jurisprudence and its succession
    2. Kelsen's theory of pure law
    3. The mediation of law through the state
    4. Hierarchy of organs and norms under the constitution
    5. Centralization and decentralization
    6. The logic of norms
    7. The various theoretizations of international law

VIII. The Immanentist Reunion of Spiritual and Secular Order
    1. Beginnings of historism in the eighteenth century
    2. The Christian gnosis of Hegel
    3. The Historical School of Law
    4. The anti-Christian gnosis of Marx
    5. The law of the immanentist church-states (Fascism, National Socialism, Russian Communism)

IX. Some Contemporary Trends in Legal Philosophy
    1. American Realism
    2. French Institutionalism
    3. Neo-Thomism

X. The End of an Epoch and the Return to the Primary Experiences of Order

3

Supplementary Notes for Students in Jurisprudence Course

LOUISIANA STATE UNIVERSITY LAW SCHOOL
1954–1957

Concerning a Rational Science of Action
1. Rational action means correct coordination of means and ends.
2. Means are relatively rational when they serve adequately the immediate purpose.
3. The full rationality of means depends on the rationality of the purpose.
4. The rationality of the purpose must be tested by interpreting it as a means to a still higher purpose.
5. If the chain of testing rationality by transforming purposes into means for higher purposes would be continued indefinitely, rationality would have no ultimate criterion.
6. Therefore: Rationality of action requires the existence of a highest good to be achieved.
7. The preceding proposition does not aver that such a highest good exists. It means that rationality of action cannot be a subject of science unless a highest good exists.
8. Application to jurisprudence: No science of jurisprudence is possible unless it is possible to develop a science of the highest good. No attempt that styles itself "jurisprudence" is science unless it contains a theory of the highest good.

Concerning the Hierarchy of Goods
1. Aristotle distinguishes three types of goods:
   A. external goods—possessions

B. goods of the body—health, strength, and beauty
C. goods of the soul—virtues

2. The virtues are distinguished as ethical and dianoetic virtues.
3. The highest good is happiness—eudaimonia.
4. The opinions concerning happiness vary among men. The three main types of preferences, according to Aristotle, are:
A. the apolaustic life
B. the political life
C. the contemplative life—*bios theoretikos*
5. Aristotle considers true happiness identical with the contemplative life.
6. The decision is based on his theory of the nature of man. Man is distinguished from other beings by his ability to develop the virtues of the soul, and specifically the dianoetic virtues. In the dianoetic virtues the nature of man comes to its full unfolding. The man who has unfolded his nature completely, through the contemplative life, is the mature man (the *spoudaios*).
7. The decision concerning true happiness, thus, is based on the science of philosophical anthropology. Nevertheless, while science furnishes objective criteria concerning true happiness (in the sense of a full unfolding of human nature), such insight does not abolish the fact that a great number of men are subjectively very happy with somewhat less than a full unfolding and would feel very miserable if they were compelled to undergo the effort of unfolding their potentialities completely. Subjective and objective happiness may coincide, but are not identical. On the other hand, the multitude of subjective opinions concerning happiness is no argument against the objective definition of happiness.

Concerning Communication

1. Paradigm: "Socrates was an Athenian." A proposition of this type, when communicated, has three dimensions of meaning:
A. the content is intended as true
B. the speaker is convinced of its truth
C. the speaker intends the listener to accept the truth into his own knowledge
2. The communication, when successful, has social

consequences, insofar as its acceptance by the listener draws
the latter into the orbit of truth as understood by the speaker.
Communication is an instrument for gaining social power
by transforming the listener into a follower of the truth
propounded by the speaker.

3. Hence, there arise difficulties with regard to free speech. If
free speech is restricted by governmental regulations
   A. the communication of truth is handicapped
   B. men are frustrated in two respects:
      (1) insofar as the communication of truth is an obligation,
      the moral personality cannot develop adequately
      (2) insofar as successful communication is an expansion of
      the individual, his way of being a power in the life of the
      community, his natural sphere of power, is restricted

4. If free speech is not restricted at all, the communication of
error has equal opportunity with the communication of truth.
If error with regard to the essentials of order in the soul and
society is communicated successfully, the result may be the
destruction of social order and the corruption of individuals.

5. The problem of free speech has no rational solution, valid
for all times. The question to what extent communication
through speech and press can be left free, or must be restricted
in certain respects, will have to be solved in the light of the
circumstances of the case.

6. Two principal solutions have been tried in the course of
Western history:
   A. radical censorship, with the instrument of inquisition, in
   the Middle Ages
   B. radical freedom (with the exception of restraints on
   obscenity, slander, and so forth) in the so-called modern,
   liberal era

7. Both solutions have failed signally:
   A. the suppression of the Middle Ages resulted in the outburst
   of the Reformation
   B. the radical modern freedom has resulted in the spread of
   totalitarian convictions that destroy the freedom under
   which they could spread

8. Conclusion: Freedom of speech and press is not a principle
of government or social order, but a prudential device for

maintaining and advancing social order, as long as it has the desired effect. Inquisitorial suppression, or thought control, is not a principle either, but again a device for maintaining social order under certain conditions.

Concerning Experiences of Transcendence

1. We can distinguish three types of civilizations:
   A. cosmological
   B. anthropological (or classical)
   C. soteriological
2. They are roughly identical with Toynbee's three generations of civilizations. The main civilizations by generations are:
   A. Egyptian, Babylonian
   B. Sinic, Indic, Israelitic, Hellenic
   C. Far Eastern (with offshoot in Japan), Hindu, Byzantine (with offshoot in Russia), Islamic, Western
3. The decisive event in the anthropological civilizations is the discovery of the psyche as the sensorium of transcendence.
4. The event is marked so sufficiently in all of the classical civilizations that one can speak of the period of 800–300 B.C. as the "axis time of mankind" (Jaspers), or as the period of transition from the "closed" to the "open" society (Bergson).
5. Nevertheless, only in Hellenic civilization has the "opening" of the soul been radical enough to result in the creation of a specific form of expression that has influenced the whole further course of Western civilization. This form is what we call "philosophy."
6. By "experience of transcendence" is meant the experience of a type of being beyond all world-immanent being.
7. Experiences of transcendence have a great variety. Heraclitus has diagnosed the three types of love, hope, and faith with regard to a world-transcendent spiritual being, the *nous*. Plato relies on *Eros*, *Thanatos*, and *Dike* as the key experiences of transcendence. Philosophy in its original meaning is love of the *sophon*, that is, of the all-wise world-transcendent being.
8. Experiences of transcendence have a large amplitude from positive to negative. Examples: love, hope, faith, trust, doubt, unbelief, anxiety, forsakenness, despair, skepticism,

indifference, active hatred, hedonistic escapes, Pascal's *divertissements*, and so forth.

9. Transcendent being—in the language of religion, God—can be identified in philosophical language variously as *nous* (Heraclitus, Aristotle), *agathon* (Plato), *logos* (Heraclitus, Stoics, Christianity), and so forth.

10. Once the soul has "opened," transcendent being becomes the source of order in community (Plato: "God is the Measure"). The order, insofar as it is constituted through orientation toward, or participation in, transcendent being, can be designated by a technical term as *homonoia* (Aristotle, Alexander, Christianity).

11. With regard to the transcendent source of order in the soul, all men are equal. The discovery of transcendent divinity as the source of order is paralleled by the discovery of mankind. "Mankind" in this sense is not a particular group of human beings at any given time, but indeed the "open society" of all men extending into the unknown future. The idea of "mankind" has nothing to do with the idea of a "world-government" established over a group of contemporaneously living human beings.

Concerning Principles of Jurisprudence

1. To the three main types of civilization correspond roughly three main types of legal cultures—roughly, because of the numerous intermediate forms.

   A. Cosmological civilizations symbolize order by analogy with cosmic order. The political community is a microcosmos. (Prototype discussed in class: early Chinese symbolism.)

   B. Anthropological civilizations symbolize order by analogy with the order of the human soul. And the order of the human soul is achieved through attunement to the unseen transcendent measure. Society is a macroanthropos. (Prototype discussed in class: Plato's conception of society as man written large.)

   C. Soteriological civilizations develop more clearly the experience of transcendent revelation and grace that reaches out to all mankind. Spiritual order is differentiated from temporal order. (Prototypes discussed in class: Israelite and Christian revelation, division into spiritual and temporal powers.)

2. In appraising the development of such widely different legal cultures in history, their meaning, and their relation among them, certain principles must be applied.

   A. First principle: Human nature is constant—by definition. Nature by definition is that which does not change. "Change of human nature" would imply that either before or after the change men are not men. The faculties and experiences of man are always present in their entirety, however different historically their expressions may look.

   B. Second principle: While human nature is constant, the self-understanding of man, with regard both to his position in the world and to transcendent reality, progresses from compactness to differentiation. What sometimes is called loosely a "change in human nature" is the advance of self-understanding from compactness to differentiation in the course of history.

   C. Third principle: Progress of self-understanding (implying the position of man within the world and with regard to transcendent reality) through differentiating experiences, and the development of symbols for their adequate expression, is an increase of knowledge. It is a progress toward rationality in the substantive sense, insofar as a more differentiated understanding of reality (including man's position in relation to transcendent reality) will make possible a more adequate coordination of means to purposes, as well as a more adequate focusing of purposes, up to the highest good to be attained. There exist, therefore, objective criteria of rationality. A Christian philosophy of law, like the Thomistic, which has a differentiated understanding of transcendent reality and places the highest good in the beatific vision through grace in death, has a high degree of rationality. A positivist, or progressivist, philosophy of law, which seeks perfection in the world-immanent course of history, has a low degree of rationality. (Discussed in class: the Kantian conflict between a Christian and a progressivist idea of perfection.)

D. Fourth principle: All legal cultures experience their primary source of order as located in transcendent reality, though the expressions of the experience differ widely according to the degrees of compactness and differentiation.

E. Fifth principle: Human experience of transcendent reality presupposes an affinity between the experiencing soul and the experienced reality. This affinity is called "consubstantiality." (Class discussion referred for the use of the term in this sense to [Frankfort,] *The Introduction to The Intellectual Adventure of Ancient Man* [Chicago, 1946].)

F. Sixth principle: The mode of cognition in the experience of transcendence is called "participation." (Examples discussed in class: the Platonic *methexis* in the *agathon*; the Thomistic *participatio* in the *ratio aeterna*.) Participation is not cognition of a world-immanent object or event, and hence cannot result in positive propositions concerning true order. Participation is a movement in the soul, a response to transcendent reality by virtue of consubstantiality. It results in a sensitiveness of the soul for injustice in the concrete situation. (Discussion in class: the Solonic struggle for translating the "unseen measure" into positive Athenian order; Plato's inability to give a positive definition of the *agathon*; the eroticism of the soul of the philosopher in the Platonic sense; the Christian definition of faith in Heb. 11 : 1.)

G. Seventh principle: Just order, since it originates in transcendent reality, cannot be defined in substantive rules. No philosophy of law can be developed as a system of rules derived from highest substantive axioms. A jurisprudence that makes this attempt must, for that reason alone, be dismissed as theoretically inadequate.

H. Eighth principle: Historical experience shows that the highest degrees of sensitive response to transcendent reality, as well as its transformation into articulate reaction against injustice in the concrete situation, are rare events. These rare events are the great lawgivers, prophets, philosophers, and saints. The development of jurisprudence as a science must proceed, therefore, through the study of the classic sources with the purpose of reenacting the experiences that have precipitated in them. This necessity must not be misunderstood as an acceptance of authority or as an occupation with the opinions of philosophers "who are long dead." It is the empirical process in which the soul of the student becomes trained in differentiated experiences; it is the gradual building of the student's soul into a sensitive instrument, by which the student can verify the truth contained in the classic sources on the problem of order. (Discussion in class: the Aristotelian conception of ethics as the science of the order in the soul of a mature man; a science that can be advanced only among mature men; and is fully intelligible only to mature men.)

I. Ninth principle: The understanding of just order progresses concretely through the reaction of a soul sensitive to the transcendent source of order against injustice in the environment. Hence the formulations of right conduct are primarily negative. (Discussion in class: the Persian Empire of Truth against the Lie; the Mosaic Decalogue of Exodus 20 with its negative injunctions; the case of Socratic ignorance; the Greek opposition of truth, *aletheia*, to falsehood, *pseudos*, from Hesiod to Plato—remember the long catalog of Platonic dichotomies.)

Concerning Natural Law

1. As "natural law" shall be understood all attempts at transforming a reaction toward injustice experienced in the concrete case into a body of fundamental, substantive rules that claim authority as expressing the true nature of man and society.

2. Natural law in this sense can develop only where a concept of human nature is formed in opposition to the accepted order of society, that is, only where man under the pressure of

80

experiences of transcendence has sufficiently differentiated from the collective existence of society.

3. In cosmological legal cultures, such a concept is not yet developed. There is usually only one category of order, designating at once divine, cosmic, social, and individual order. Examples discussed in class: the Chinese category of *tao*, the Egyptian category of *maat*. The ruler of a cosmological empire (the Chinese Son of Heaven, the Egyptian Pharaoh) serves as the transformer of divine and cosmic order into social and individual order. Only in the crisis of a cosmological empire (Toynbee's Time of Troubles) arises the problem of individual transformation of cosmic order into order in the soul of the individual man, without mediation by the public representative. Typical case: Confucius.

4. Aristotle distinguishes natural and legal justice. A social order is built according to natural justice if it furnishes the suitable environment for the full unfolding of human potentialities to the *bios theoretikos* of the mature man (*Nic. Ethics* V; and *Politics* VII–VIII).

5. Thomas understands natural law as the insights into right order that are possible to man by virtue of his participation in the *lex aeterna*. These insights are imperfect and must be aided by the revealed *lex divina*.

6. The opposition of a right order by nature to the concrete order of a society is a revolutionary act. One variety of natural law can, therefore, be distinguished as revolutionary natural law.

7. A revolutionary opposition to an existing order, if successful, may endanger the existence of a society. In reaction to the primary natural law, therefore, frequently we find a secondary natural law that stresses as natural the historically grown order of a society. This secondary law may be called conservative natural law.

8. In appraising the value of systems of natural law, the following criteria must be used:
   A. Natural law has theoretical justification insofar as it translates the insights gained by a theory of the nature of man into the language of obligatory purposes. As example

may serve the Aristotelian translation: by theoretical insight the *bios theoretikos* is the full unfolding of human potentiality. Translated into a moral rule: man should strive to find this fulfillment in his personal existence. Rule of natural justice: society should be organized in such a manner that the fulfillment of the purpose is possible, at least for those who wish to attain it.

B. Natural law becomes dubious if it erects theoretically justified, paradigmatic rules of order into postulates of revolutionary reform. Aristotle was very outspoken on the point that his creation of a paradigmatic right order of society in *Politics* VII–VIII was not a recipe for reforming the Hellenic polis. His recipes for concrete action, in *Politics* IV–VI, were of an entirely different, Machiavellian nature.

C. Natural law is worthless if it contains no more than partisan preferences without a basis in a critical theory of the nature of man.

9. In periods of spiritual and moral crisis in a society, there arises a specific kind of natural law that attempts to construct the order of a society out of contractual relations between the members of the society. The origin of this type of contract theory was analyzed by Plato in the *Republic*. It originates in the conception of man as a being that is motivated by passions alone. The order among human beings that exists by virtue of *homonoia*, that is, by virtue of their common participation in transcendent reality, is not recognized as existent. The withdrawal of man from participation in the common *nous* into the shell of his passions was characterized by Heraclitus as the creation of a private dream-world in opposition to the public world of participation in the *koinon*, the common *nous*. Plato resumes the Heraclitian idea of the dream-worlds of individual passion. Out of such individual dream-worlds no common order can be constructed because the agreement lacks the obligatory force that stems from participation in the common transcendent reality. The contracts would be empty formulae. This analysis is valid for all later constructions of a similar type.

10. The type of contract theory analyzed by Plato must be distinguished from the theories that let social order arise from a "social instinct." The "social instinct" is a compact symbol, of little theoretical value once the differentiated analysis of the origins of order has been established. But it is not guilty of the fallacy described in the preceding paragraph.

4

Right and Might

Professor James Brown Scott's two volumes are an outstanding achievement in the dogmatic literature on the subjects of law and international order.[1] Professor Scott is representative of that school of thought that isolates the legal order from the context of social and political reality and treats it as if it were a realm in itself to be established sooner or later on this earth after certain obstacles have been overcome in the course of evolution. Once we accept this premise, it becomes a sensible enterprise to inquire into the nature and structure of the evolving order and to "codify" it systematically, as Professor Scott does in Volume II of his great work. Under three headings—Jurisprudence, The State, The Law of Nations— he gives a well-ordered collection of quotations from the leading authorities since the Greeks on the elements of the desired order. While Volume II presents a systematic codification of principles and rules as evolved through the consent of authorities, Volume I is a historical "Commentary" on the development of the system as set forth in the *codex*. And the Introduction to Volume I "brings to the reader's attention certain conceptions of law and society which are at once fundamental and almost universally accepted."

The work has the avowed purposes of codifying a system and of supporting it by the authority of congenial thinkers. All I can do, therefore, is to bring out some of the leading axioms of its con-

This review appeared originally in *The Review of Politics*, III (1941), 122–23. Reprinted with permission.

1. James Brown Scott, *Law, the State, and the International Community* (New York, 1939). Vol. I: *A Commentary on the Development of Legal, Political, and International Ideas.* Vol. II: *Extracts Illustrating the Growth of Theories and Principles of Jurisprudence, Government, and the Law of Nations.*

ception. The first is the thesis that there is, indeed, an evolution through the history of mankind of ideas and institutions towards the aim of a peaceful order of law. This first axiom necessitates a number of others. As the history of mankind is quite obviously not a unit of straight evolution but presents the picture of coordinated civilizations such as the Far Eastern, the Mesopotamian, the Western, and the Arabic, the concept of the "historic era" has to be introduced in order to reach a basis for the system. The "historic era" begins with the fifth century B.C. in Greece and extends from this starting point through Western history up to the present, absorbing on its way the Hebrew prophets and Christianity. Minor items like China, India, Egypt, and the Byzantine Empire are apparently relegated with the Primitives to the limbo of prehistory. Even [with] the restriction [of the history of mankind] to the "historic era," however, the stream of evolution does not flow quite smoothly. The gaps between the high points have either to be ignored or to be explained as deviations and temporary retrogressions. The literature of the Great Migration is ignored entirely; there is a desert of eight centuries from Saint Augustine to John of Salisbury, relieved only by Saint Isidore of Sevilla and the *Decretum Gratianum*. With the Renaissance, then, begins the appearance of doubtful personalities such as Machiavelli and Bodin who do not contribute much, if anything, to the order of law and, therefore, are barred from being quoted in Volume II. And after Hooker and Grotius, evolution evolves so badly that nobody at all is quoted any more. By judicious omission of this sort, a solid chain of straightforward evolution is forged, stretching from Plato and Aristotle, over Cicero, the *Codex Justinianus*, Saint Augustine, Saint Thomas Aquinas, Vitoria, and Suarez, to Hooker and Grotius.

I could imagine that even a convinced adherent of Professor Scott's ideas might experience some uneasiness when he labors through the honest and scholarly Commentary. It might occur to him that the great contributions towards an order of law have an unhappy inclination to coincide with periods of history that are far from representing the ideal of a peaceful and just order: that the Stoic contribution, for example, marks the decay of Hellas and the sanguinary conquest of Asia by Alexander; that the Ciceronian contribution marks the beginning of the not-altogether-peaceful Roman conquest; and that the beginning of modern international law in the sixteenth century coincides with the Spanish conquest of America. There seems to be a connection between the idea of order and the existence of a power to maintain it. While Professor Scott is certainly justified in asserting frequently that might does not make right, it is unfortunately equally true that it makes an order, and that without it an order can be neither created nor maintained. Here is perhaps the point where the intrinsic inconsistency of an attitude that tends to separate the idea of order from the realities of power becomes obvious. Because the possession of power does not grant the righteousness of the order maintained by it, power and the application of force frequently are found to be immoral in themselves. It seems to be one of the most difficult things for a political thinker to separate clearly the problem of the contents of an order from the problem of enforcing it. The question of right enters into the principles on which an order is built; the maintenance of an order will have always, human nature being what it is, to rely on the instrument of force.

5

Two Recent Contributions to the Science of Law

An adequate science of law has no simple object. It is not exhausted by a history of institutions or a blueprint of a just order, nor by an analysis of the logical structure of legal rules nor by a classification of social behavior, nor by an inquiry into power structures nor by an analysis of the judicial process. It ranges from the biological characteristics of man to the ethical and religious background of a civilization, from the economic system of a community to the logic of normative judgments, from the expansiveness of the human being (symbolized in the concept of liberty) and its shrinking in anxiety (symbolized in the concept of fear) to delicate technical discussions on the best way of achieving a certain social end by means of regulation. None of these topics is unimportant in a full presentation of the object, none of them can be neglected as only incidental; every one of them requires the full mastery of the materials as well as of the methods employed in their interpretation. This picture of the problem is, I think, the result of roughly a century and a half of the great contributions made to the science of law through the different approaches of analytical, historical, philosophical, and sociological jurisprudence. It is on the background of this result that we have to place two important recent contributions to the science of law: Professor Timasheff's *Sociology of Law* and Professor Bodenheimer's *Jurisprudence*.[1]

It seems to be significant for the high quality of the work of the

This review appeared originally in *The Review of Politics*, III (1941), 399–404. Reprinted with permission.
1. N. S. Timasheff, *An Introduction to the Sociology of Law*, Harvard Sociological Studies, III (Cambridge, Mass., 1940); Edgar Bodenheimer, *Jurisprudence* (New York, 1939).

two scholars that though they differ considerably in their method of approach, they coincide to a high degree in their treatment of the subject. The agreement is due to the fact that they both accept essentially the situation just outlined and do not try to narrow down the topic again to any one of its component parts. Both are characterized by the catholicity of outlook that prevents an unduly one-sided emphasis on either the historical, the analytical, the political, or the ethical aspect. They agree that law is not an aprioric structure of the human mind nor, therefore, a phenomenon to be found invariably at all stages of civilization, but that it has a historical status. And they agree that the most satisfactory way to arrive at a definition of law is, therefore, to form an ideal type of the fully developed stage and to characterize other types of community order through their differences from the mature type of law. This concurrence of opinion on the general premises leaves, however, ample room for profound divergence in the organization of the materials; and the two books are representative, not only through their agreement but also through their differences, of scientific techniques that show clearly the present difficulties in the way of a further development of the science of law.

Law is defined by Professor Timasheff as an "ethico-imperative coordination of behavior," meaning thereby an order that "is constituted by patterns of conduct enforced by agents of centralized power (tribunals and administration) and simultaneously supported by a group-conviction that the corresponding conduct 'ought to be'" (17). Law, understood in this way, "is not a necessary form of human existence, not a category of human thought," but "a historical phenomenon, a product of cultural development" (272). These definitions determine the organization of the book. Part I is an introduction that explains the general place of a sociology of law in science. Parts II and III deal with the two component elements of law, Ethics and Power respectively, and Part IV deals with that overlapping section of ethical and power problems that the author has defined as Law. Within the three main parts (II to IV), the subject matter is organized under the chief captions of Equilibrium, Change, Differentiation and Integration, and Disintegration of the socio-ethical situation, the power structure and the institutions of law. Practically all of the topics that are cataloged above have found a place under one of these headings. On this point we have to say only that Professor Timasheff offers a competent and eminently useful survey of the field, based on a broad knowledge of the literature on the subject, and that the book is an excellent and readable introduction to the problem.

There arise, however, certain difficulties that are due to the methodological position adopted by Professor Timasheff. From the above catalog of problems it seems obvious that the complex phenomenon of law cannot be mastered monistically by just one method selected at random, but that the different elements involved require their peculiar and widely differing methods in order to be treated adequately. This necessity is neglected by Professor Timasheff, for he is an adherent of the positivistic notion of science and, in particular, assumes that "sociology is a nomographic science" (19). This somewhat dictatorial statement, made by Professor Timasheff without an attempt at justification, hampers the adequate organization of the field. Even within the field of sociology proper in the narrowest sense, the position is questionable, because the actual methods employed by sociologists are far from being "nomographic." The "ideal types," for instance, are neither descriptive of "uniformities in society in the form of natural laws," nor are they historical idiographic concepts, but they belong to a complicated third class of conceptual instruments, described in detail by Max Weber. The dichotomy of nomographic and idiographic sciences, as developed by Windelband and Rickert, seems to me to have been untenable for thirty-five years if it is meant to be exhaustive. Of course, Professor Timasheff does not follow his own methodological precepts. His definition of law quoted above is not nomographic but a more or less well-constructed type concept, and this fact cannot be glossed over by his treating the concept as if it were a law of gravitation, the validity of which has to be verified by experiments. Professor Timasheff sets himself the task of "proving" that law is, indeed, an ethico-imperative coordination of social behavior, after he has bluntly asserted that it is one. I confess, I do not see how a type concept can be "proven." It is developed on the basis of materials that seem to be relevant for one reason or another, and it is developed in order to fit them. It would be a great surprise if it did not fit the materials that gave rise to its formation. Professor Timasheff, being a competent and skillful scientist, has, of course, evolved his concept on the basis of his knowledge of the materials, and it does not make much sense to pretend that the concept has fallen from heaven and now miraculously fits the social phenomenon. It would, however, be of prime importance to discuss the materials and to explain why they are considered to be relevant and why certain essential features should enter into the formation of the type concept; but this question of relevance is entirely omitted by Professor Timasheff.

While it would be the proper procedure to present the materials first in an introductory way and to discuss the question of relevance, it would in some cases perhaps not matter very much for the concrete scientific results whether the types are covered by a façade of nomographic epistemology. In the case of Professor Timasheff's topic, however, the "natural law" fiction results in a rigidity of construction that is incompatible with the complexity of the object. His type concept of law may be a good abbreviation of the relevant elements, and one may agree that the elements of regulation—order, ethical group consent, and imposition through governmental agencies—should enter into the concept, but that does not imply that the type can become the sufficient basis for a systematic scientific treatment of law. Besides ethical conviction and power imposition there enter into the subject the topics mentioned above, and several more, on an equal footing. To subdivide the field into ethics, power, and law means that one has to cram a wealth of problems that do not come under any of these headings into the wrong systematic places and, consequently, to warp the proportions of the problems considerably. And it is furthermore rather a *tour de force* to subsume topics, ranging from the ontology of the human being to the concretization of legal rules through judicial decisions, under such headings as equilibrium, change, integration and differentiation. At this point the author's insistence on treating the phenomenon of law at all cost under the idea of "nomographic sociology" interferes seriously with the success of an otherwise brilliantly started enterprise. It might be worthwhile to consider again an occasional remark of Max Weber's that the departmental division of a university does not reflect the structure of the universe; and while there are sound reasons for having departments of sociology, this does not imply that the phenomenon of law, being a social phenomenon, can be adequately treated under categories that at some time or other have been called sociological. The present situation of the science of law, as outlined above, and as implicitly accepted by Professor Timasheff, requires a scholar who is a sociologist, a psychologist, a political scientist, a lawyer, and a good metaphysician on top. If it were necessary at all to give a proof of the honest scholarly work of Professor Timasheff, it would be sufficient to point to the fact that his somewhat departmental approach to the topic did not deter him from treating the problems of the field in their whole breadth. It is not the least of his contributions to have revealed by this contradiction, which pervades his book, the true nature of the problem.

Professor Bodenheimer's *Jurisprudence* presents an interesting contrast to Professor Timasheff's *Sociology of Law*. While Professor Timasheff has an abstract and systematic mind to the degree that he opens his book with definitions of concepts without revealing how he arrived at them and why he puts them forward, then passes on and finds to his agreeable surprise that they fit reality and have not been introduced in vain after all, leaving his reader to ponder on the miracle of the prestabilized harmony, Professor Bodenheimer starts from the object as it occurs in history and tries to penetrate from the obvious occurrence to the elements that may have entered into the composition of the complex result. The titles that he gives to the four parts of his book should, therefore, not be understood as descriptive of a system, but rather as the names of the provocative stimuli for a science of law that may be found in the historical environment. Part I deals with Power and Law and includes a chapter on Justice, obviously assembled not for systematic reasons but for their topical connection in everyday discourse on the subject. Part II deals with the Law of Nature, again not a systematic elemental unit, but a historical occurrence of complex structure. Part III on the Law-shaping Forces, including political, psychological, economic, national, racial, and cultural factors, comes nearest to a systematic survey. And Part IV, dealing with Positivism in Jurisprudence, singles out for special treatment the analytical and positivistic sociological theories of the nineteenth century and after. Professor Bodenheimer does not give any reasons for this organization of the material, though it might be worthwhile to give it some consideration.

As law, in the opinion of both of the authors, is not an aprioric structure but at least partially a socio-historical phenomenon, the question arises, as observed earlier, as to the criterion for a scientifically relevant selection of materials out of a diffuse field. The positivistic approach of Professor Timasheff simply dodges this question; Professor Bodenheimer gives a practical selection but does not justify it. The first delimitation of relevant units in the case of law is given in the self-interpretation of historical reality through the persons who express their metaphysical, political, and ethical preferences in a given situation; that is, relevant is, in the first approach, what the members of legally ordered communities think to be relevant. If we wish to delimit a phenomenon like law, we have to begin with an investigation into the thought of the persons engaged in shaping the order of their community as humble members through their everyday conduct and opinion, as politicians and professional and systematic thinkers. Such thought materials can be only a starting point because they are pragmatic, and one has to proceed to the elements entering into this type of materials, but they are after all our only avenue to a relevant selection. It is, therefore, scientifically highly commendable to group the materials around the main types and trends of pragmatic thought as Professor Bodenheimer does, though this grouping of materials is the first and not the last effort of a science of law.

This approach seems to be particularly congenial to the author, because he himself has a purpose of his own in shaping his system, the purpose bringing out the limiting function of law. He defines that "Law in its purest and most perfect form will be realized in a social order in which the possibility of abuse of power by private individuals as well as by the government is reduced to a minimum" (19). Law in this sense has the function of limiting the actions of the individuals to behavior patterns that are mutually compatible with one another, and it limits the actions of rulers so that the plain members of the community may be reasonably secure against unexpected, arbitrary governmental interference in their private spheres. This accent on the limiting function draws the borders of the field of law somewhat narrower than Professor Timasheff's definition, and Professor Bodenheimer makes it a point that the group consent as introduced by Professor Timasheff might support an arbitrary dictatorial unlimited rule. It may be a question whether this narrower definition is in the best accord with the self-interpretation of social reality—which is the ultimate instance in this matter—but Professor Bodenheimer can certainly advance good reasons for working out his ideal type on the model of the Western constitutional governments. And besides, it does not matter very much scientifically as long as the actual differences of the types are brought out carefully, though it matters very much practically to Professor Bodenheimer, who wishes to monopolize the term *law* for constitutional governments and to deny it to the legal order of dictatorships.

As the author approaches the problem of Jurisprudence through pragmatic thought on the subject matter, the bulk of the book is a report of doctrines on the several aspects of law. Even if one should have some doubts as to the ultimate systematic value of the book, it stands as an excellent, cleverly arranged history of the theory of law and may be used to advantage as a text on this subject matter. The survey of Stoic, Christian, Classic, and Modern Natural Law (103–92) and the survey of the literature on the law-shaping forces (195–261) are particularly competent introductions into these fields. The treatment assumes the form of a short and, on the whole, correct report of the theories, followed by concise and pertinent critical remarks that lead beyond the theories in question into the systematic problems—though not very far. This method has the advantage of outlining the present situation of the science of law, resulting in a picture similar to that drawn in my introductory remarks, but it has the disadvantages of hampering the development of constructive ideas, because the argument is linked too closely to the traditional treatment of the problems. Systematically, therefore, those sections are more fruitful that analyze such thinkers as had a comprehensive philosophical education—that is, to the end of the eighteenth century—while the result becomes somewhat barren when the survey enters upon the period of the beginning division of labor in the social sciences, and particularly in the report on the great lawyer literature on law that developed in the nineteenth century.

Lawyers are a noble and arrogant race. Filled with understandable pride by the practical importance of their profession, they all too frequently believe that if they master the law dogmatically, they are sufficiently equipped to deal with it scientifically—which they are not. To watch some of the great nineteenth-century authorities on Roman Law when they develop the juridical concept of *res* on the basis of the meaning of "thing" in "natural science" is a hair-raising experience. And even when they condescend to acquire some knowledge of the methods employed in science, this knowledge and its application remain frequently dilettantic. The parochial flavor of this period has entered somewhat into Professor Bodenheimer's account of it. I think, however, that it was important to clarify the situation, and when Professor Bodenheimer concludes his book programmatically by pointing to the need of combining the methods of the several approaches to the science of law in order to arrive at a complete and adequate treatment of this highly complex subject matter, he at least has made it plain beyond doubt where we stand at present, and he has also demonstrated that for the future a science of law has to be built on a complete mastery of its several branches.

6

The Theory of Legal Science: A Review

I

The number of contributions to a theory of legal science is so small that every essay in the field can be assured of eager attention. The present monograph of Mr. Cairns can be assured of it doubly because of the qualities of the author as well as of his work.[1] To give an adequate account of the compact book is, however, not an easy task. There are several circumstances that baffle the reader; I shall report them first without comment, and only afterwards venture on an evaluation of the problems presented by the author.

Mr. Cairns intends to give a theory of legal science. Normally, a reader who opens a book bearing this title would expect to find in it set forth the epistemology and methodology of a science that actually exists, even if its theoretical foundations should have remained hitherto unsatisfactory; one would expect the author to point to the body of knowledge of which he purports to clarify the theoretical principles. In this respect the reader will be disappointed. For Mr. Cairns is of the opinion that legal science does not exist at all, if we except a few honorable fragments, and that its creation is a task for the future. The book contains, therefore, on the whole, the theory of a non-existent science.

The science does not exist, but in the opinion of the author it should exist. In order to aid it in coming into being, he undertakes the maieutic work of outlining its aims and its basic theoretical

This review appeared originally in *Louisiana Law Review*, IV (1942), 554–71. Reprinted with permission.

1. Huntington Cairns, *The Theory of Legal Science* (Chapel Hill, N.C., 1941).

problems; and then he invites us to get busy on it. Some readers may become irritated by the author's way of telling people what to do instead of doing it himself; but such irritation would not be quite justified. There is certainly an exhortatory tone running through the book that occasionally makes the reader feel that the author might legitimate his theoretical undertaking somewhat by carrying out a few of the things that apparently he knows should be done. But there is more to the work than just exhortation. The discussion has a positive value because, in the review of past approaches, it reveals theoretical fallacies and factual mistakes to be avoided in future; in addition, the author suggests what he believes to be the principal problem of a legal science—and as we shall see, the problem suggested is indeed the crucial problem of any science of social order. The delimitation of a field of science through the formulation of its central problem is certainly an important theoretical achievement; but the mere formulation leaves us completely in the dark about the content of the future science. This situation makes the book difficult reading. Its style is clear (with the exception of one or two obscure passages) and the development of the problems is lucid. But throughout the book the unfortunate reader is unable to refer the ideas of the author to any fact of science, especially because the author assures him at every turn that there is none and that it will require patient work of generations of scholars to produce the science. The reader is continuously floundering and hesitating in his understanding because he is supposed not to know what the author is talking about.

This, however, is only the predicament of the lay reader who is willing to trust the author unconditionally. The expert in the field will find another reason to be baffled. Mr. Cairns gives after all some indications (very sparingly) of the scope and purpose of the future legal science. Negatively, he makes it clear that legal science is not legal history; that it cannot exhaust itself in the mere accumulation of facts (no more descriptive institutionalism) but has to formulate general rules; that it is not identical with analytical jurisprudence of the Austinian type; that current schools of legal theory such as sociological jurists, realists, and experimentalists come under the title of "legal technology"; and that their results cannot be the basis of a science, important as their work may be in other respects. Positively, he defines legal science as the science of human behavior that has for its function the elimination of disorder and the creation of order in society (2). Legal science in this sense does not deal with the institutions of civil and criminal law only, but includes a large part at least of the subject matter of political science (3). This rather large field, which potentially might include all kinds of human behavior productive of order, is narrowed in later passages by the enumeration of six elements of legal structure that are to constitute the principal field of inquiry. The six elements are persons, associations, property, promises, the constitution of the community, and the sustaining administrative system (93). For the sake of abbreviating the classification, the author shows a tendency to bring the six elements under three headings: the regulation of behavior (including the first four elements), the constitution, and the administrative system (98). The delimitation of the field to six (or three) elements is further supplemented by the definition of law as the means of social control "which, for its enforcement, embodies in itself, or has behind it, a definite agency which exerts, or through which may be exerted, the pressure of politically organized society" (22). Mr. Cairns is aware that this definition is oriented toward the modern state and that the inclusion of other legal systems would have to take proper account of "equivalents" to the enforcement machinery evolved by the modern state (23). The ultimate aim of a science exploring this field will be the formulation of a system of general rules; but before rules of high generality can be formulated, we have to prepare the way by the provisional construction of ideal types. "Ideal entities embodying the orders of legal relations take us to the relevant in the enormous varieties of social life and permit us to make comparisons which may possibly lead to generalization and ultimately to knowledge, universality and system" (111).

The program is laudable and I have no criticism to offer at this stage; but as I said, the expert reader will be baffled by it. The project of a legal science as a social science dealing with human behavior oriented towards the problem of order in general, as well as the classification of the three orders (regulation, administration, constitution), the definition of law by reference to the enforcing agent, and above all the project of proceeding through the construction of ideal types, are features familiar to the reader because they are singly and in combination closely related to the sociological principles of Max Weber. The name of Max Weber appears in the monograph of Mr. Cairns only once in a reference to his *Protestant Ethic and the Spirit of Capitalism* (which is translated into English). That Max Weber is the creator of a system of sociology based on the construction of ideal types, that he has expounded the theoretical principles of the science at considerable length in essays that have become classics of methodology, and that in 1922 his posthumous (fragmentary) treatise on *Wirtschaft und Gesellschaft* was published, seems to be entirely unknown to Mr. Cairns. The treatise on *Wirtschaft und Gesellschaft* is a quarto volume in small print that would run in ordinary book-size into more than two thousand pages, half of which are devoted to the execution of precisely the project that is now suggested by Mr. Cairns. We are faced by the curiosity of a treatise trying to evolve from scratch, with considerable labor, a theoretical position that was developed with great precision several decades ago in all its details and supplemented with more than a thousand pages of rich material application. It would be highly unfair, however, to assume that Mr. Cairns does not know about Max Weber; on the contrary, he quotes one of his works. Max Weber is, furthermore, known to every scholar in the field as a towering giant in the social science of the last generation; his work is available in every major library; and his fundamental concepts have been submitted to an acute analysis by Professor Talcott Parsons in his *Structure of Social Action*. The attitude of Mr. Cairns is enigmatic and cannot be explained, perhaps, by anyone but himself. Anyway, the reader who is interested in the suggestions of Mr. Cairns is referred to the work of Max Weber as the standard treatise on the "legal science" that, according to Mr. Cairns, does not exist.

Some readers may consider the case closed once this point has become clear. But again, the conclusion would be hasty. The assumptions made by the author with regard to the state of legal science are incorrect. Legal science, in his sense of the term, exists weightily (and not only in the work of Max Weber, I may add), and its theoretical problems are elaborated far beyond any point reached by the author. We have to discount these facts in dealing with the book under review. For Mr. Cairns is a philosophical personality in his own right, and what an original philosophical mind of his quality has to say deserves attention without regard to the situation just outlined. Social science still has to operate under handicaps; and the endeavors of the author, in their successes and their failures, offer revealing insights into the theoretical situation of our time. If in the following critical evaluation of the author's positions the shortcomings seem to outweigh the achievements, the reader should not be induced to underrate the contribution of Mr. Cairns. To see the problems at all and to be concerned about them is the most important step in their treatment.

II

The first question that has to be clarified concerns the model of science underlying the theoretical analysis. The question is of particular importance in the context of the book because legal science supposedly does not exist and the creation of its model is the prelude to its future material elaboration. With regard to this problem, Mr. Cairns seems to submit in a considerable degree to the "superstition of science," that is, to the belief that the natural sciences offer the model for the social sciences. The natural sciences are the "more successful" sciences and we should do our best to reach similar prosperity (11). The specific ideals held up in pursuit of success are 1) the generality of laws (7), 2) the predictability of events on the basis of general laws (10), and 3) exactness (139).

Let us take up the last point first. The author does not define *exactness*, but from the context it appears that he opposes the "more exact" sciences to the "less rigorous" studies (139). This pair of terms may be considered of doubtful value. If "exactness" has any theoretical meaning at all, if applied to physics as the model science, it can only mean that laws of physics are formulated mathematically. The use, however, of the formal apparatus of mathematics in the couching of propositions in any science is a matter not of choice but of ontological possibility. We operate with mathematical symbols in the formulation of propositions concerning time-space-mass relations because we *can* apply them to relations in this realm of being. We do not apply mathematical symbols to the "anatomy of revolutions" or the "routinization of charisma" because the structure of the subject matter does not permit their application. The attempt to apply mathematical methods to phenomena of the class just mentioned would not make the propositions exact but would result in nonsense. As soon as we realize that the "inexactness" of the social sciences simply means that the specific structure of subject matter requires other methods than the mathematical, the idea of keeping up with the Joneses will lose its appeal; we shall realize that "legal science" has its own standards of precision, though their infinitely higher complexity makes it much more difficult to maintain them or to reach an opinion, in the individual case, as to whether they have been observed or not.

The second ideal of science, the formulation of general rules, is rather obscure. Mr. Cairns expresses it as follows: the object of legal science must be "to ascertain if the complex reality of the phenomena with which it is concerned exhibits elements of orderly recurrence which may be formulated in terms of generalizations or specific laws" (13). This ideal he opposes to the unsatisfactory state of a "mere accumulation of facts" (13). In the light of the third ideal, that of the predictability of consequences of social actions (10), the passage quoted seems to mean that general rules are rules stating that the social phenomenon A whenever it occurs will be followed regularly in time by the social phenomenon B. But the intentions of the author are not quite clear on this point. On other occasions he speaks of general laws "which unite a number of particular facts" (7) or of "invariant relationships among the facts" (10), without any reference to a time sequence; these formulae might apply as well to typical structural configurations. The unclearness of the formulae cannot be relieved by reference to specific instances of laws because the author, taking very seriously his assumption that legal science does not exist, does not give any. As the author leaves us groping in the dark, he will not object, I hope, if we base our comments on a mere impression: we have the feeling that his predominant model of generality is the recurrence of time-sequences of social phenomena.

This postulate of general rules, if we have understood it correctly, obviously involves serious questions. It is formulated in imitation of the structure of "natural sciences" (7 f.); the problem arises, therefore, whether the subject matter of social order has the same structure as the subject matter of inorganic nature. The problem is slurred over by Mr. Cairns through his frequent use of the term *external world* for both nature and society; but this use involves a *petitio principii*: whether there is an external world with a uniform structure of subject matter is precisely the point in question. The author himself has his qualms about the omnipresence of general rules, but he assuages them by the sentence: "The ideal remains warranted in the absence of a demonstration—which is still to be offered—that its realization is impossible" (8). This is a neat trick of shoving the proof to the opponent, but it does not hold water. The author, who so amply quotes methodological literature, should know that a negative proposition concerning facts cannot be proved according to the rules of verifiability that he himself sets forth so ably in his book (70). If he is waiting for a demonstration of the impossibility of general rules in legal science, he will have a long time to wait, because it cannot be given.

The problem of the structure of social science lies elsewhere. Mr. Cairns states rightly that the ideal of science "determines in large part the subject matter to be selected for examination, the methods to be adopted, even the facts which will be chosen for study" (8). In brief, the question of relevance and of the principle of selection is the crucial question with regard to the structure of social science. On the question of relevance the book, however, is silent, except for its enumeration of topics, which has previously been noticed; and it is silent for the good reason that Mr. Cairns has no overt philosophy of man and of his place in society and the world at large that could tell him what is relevant in the world of man and society. The whole branch of knowledge that goes today under the name of philosophical anthropology is non-existent for the author. Unless we have an idea of man, we have no frame of reference for the designation of human phenomena as relevant or irrelevant. Man is engaged in the creation of social order physically, biologically, psychologically, intellectually, and spiritually. Some of these engagements will offer the opportunity for the formulation of fairly general rules: for example, a societal order based on monastic ideals and on the postulate of celibacy will die out within a generation unless it can recruit itself from a surrounding society; or, no society is stable if the ruling class is not the wealthiest class through personal property or through the institutionalized chance of disposition over the wealth of the country; or, a movement under charismatic leadership will become institutionalized or disintegrate rapidly. Other propositions will apply to certain cultural areas only, as for instance, Calvinism is a contributing factor in the formation of rational working habits. And some propositions can hardly be called general at all because there is only one case involved, as for instance, the idea of the equality of men in the Western world is partly shaped by Christianity.

Faced by the fact of social science as it appears from these scanty examples, it seems somewhat futile to lay down the law that legal science should be a body of rules of a certain type. Our first concern is with the relevance of subject matter: if social phenomena appear to us as relevant, they will become the object of scientific investigation, and we shall try to form ideal types of structures, factors, time-sequences, et cetera, as the necessity arises without bothering much about their degree of generality. The town, for instance, as a form of ordered social life may seem relevant to us; and then we shall set about to construct the types of Hellenic, oriental, Mesopotamian, medieval, and modern occidental towns, and we shall not be deterred from such undertaking because the "ideal type" of the medieval town is not a "general rule" and has no chance of leading us to further general rules (111). Of course, Mr. Cairns might object that he is not interested in scientific propositions that do not lead, at least, to general rules. Confronted by this argument we would have to give up: nobody is obliged to be interested in any particular science or in science at all. If the author should not be interested in social science as it exists, that would be his private affair; he certainly would have no authority to declare the rather impressive results of social science as non-existent or unscientific because and insofar as they do not correspond to his idea of generality. A proposition may be illegitimate in a system of social science for one of two reasons: 1) because it is unverifiable, or 2) because it is irrelevant in the system of reference that is determined by philosophical anthropology; the question of generality has no bearing on the legitimacy of its status.

III

The last sentences seem to mark a limit of theoretical discussion—but the reader will have noticed the conditional. There is no disagreement between Mr. Cairns and other social scientists on the point that propositions have to be verifiable and that type-constructions have to fit the facts. The point of potential disagreement appears in the theory of relevance. Obviously, we do not all have the same idea of man and our principles of selection of relevant subject matter may differ widely. The great systems of social thought have different rules of relevance because they have different anthropologies. The anthropology of Aristotle is not that of Plato, the Machiavellian is not the Thomistic, the Bodinian not the Hobbesian, and so forth; and the systems of these thinkers are at variance with each other less because of disagreement about facts than because of disagreement about anthropological principles. If this is the theoretical situation, do we have to accept the consequence that there never will be a social science in steady progress to ever higher perfection of the system like the natural sciences? Will social science be at the mercy of any individual position with regard to metaphysical questions about the nature of man? The answer is an emphatic yes.

Let us reduce the first shock somewhat by the assurance that the situation is not in danger of degenerating into chaotic subjectivism; above all, the weight of the social institutions surrounding us is a corrective to aberrations, insofar as the idea of man embodied in them will influence the amplitude of the socially possible disagreement. The errors of philosophical anthropology within this established frame are, furthermore, permanently under corrective discussion. Anyone who would build today a science of social order on the assumption that the creation and content of social order are not influenced by the religious consciousness of man and by his religious ideas, or on the assumption that economic problems are not a factor in political order, or that certain elements of human nature that are studied by mass psychology can be neglected, will not find much admiration for his subjective achievement; he will be told politely but firmly to get acquainted with the facts of life before he starts talking about problems of social order. Through all disagreement among philosophers, there is a convergence towards standards that makes it impossible to claim the successful construction of a system unless the anthropology underlying it gives due weight to the various elements of human nature.

While there exists a certain stock of knowledge about man that a scholar in the field of social science is not at liberty to disregard grossly without exposing himself to the reproach of incompetence, there is no hope of steady improvement by concerted efforts. For the idea of man is not a datum of the external world but a creation of the human spirit, undergoing historical changes, and it has to be recreated by every generation and by every single person. To mention the most decisive epoch of the idea: the appearance of Christ has added to the idea of man the dimension of the spiritual singularity of every human being, so that we can no longer build a science of social order, for instance, on the anthropologies of Plato or Aristotle. Likewise, within the Christian Western world the idea of man is not static but changes constantly; it has acquired, for instance, through and since the Renaissance the dimension of historic singularity. The chief determinants of the various ideas are to be found in the fundamental religious attitudes of the thinkers who created and transformed them. The physical and social sciences differ, therefore, profoundly in their epistemologies. The realm of matter is, in a sense, static, and the progress we can make in its explorations is the progress in the dissection of a corpse that holds still; the realm of man and society is relatively much more alive and the degree of understanding will be determined by the amplitude of the idea of man that is at the disposition of a scholar through environmental tradition and through the breadth of his personality. Consequently we have to be extremely cautious in attributing the deficiencies of an effort in the social sciences to plain lack of knowledge (which, of course, also occurs quite frequently); if there is any doubt, we should rather attribute the selections and omissions to the fundamental attitude of a scholar with regard to the idea of man.

After this digression we can now return to the preferences of Mr. Cairns. His idea of general rules is not just a private fancy, and the discussion is not at an end. We have to deal now with the ideas of man and society implied in the author's monograph. In this analysis we have to tread very cautiously, because the discussion cannot be straightforward. Mr. Cairns does not develop an idea of man explicitly and we have to infer his idea from the implications of his statements. The most important step in its understanding is done through the very recognition of the fact that it is only implied. The nature of man does not become explicitly problematical, because the author does not take his stand in the realm of experiences that determine the religious and historical singularity of the person.

Mr. Cairns knows that there is a problem of relevance, but he does not see that relevancies change with the idea of man and that this idea has its roots in the sphere of self-reflective personality, in which the attitudes of man toward the world are constituted. He assumes that there is only one legitimate system of relevancies and that the problem, therefore, needs no discussion. And he can make this assumption because man is for him a part of the external world, along with other natural phenomena, seen from the outside. Whole sections of the human person that have decisive functions in the constitution of social order do not enter, therefore, his field of observation. At this point it becomes difficult to decide whether some of the surprising statements of Mr. Cairns should be excused as being the expression of his peculiar idea of man, or whether a more critical approach would be justified. I select a passage characteristic of his attitude towards religious phenomena. For instance, we find the sentence: "In the tradition of Christianity, a knowledge of truth was a necessary element in salvation, but knowledge which was not religious was heretical" (131). The sentence is supported, in a footnote, by the authority of Gibbon. May I suggest that the author read the *Prooemium* of Thomas Aquinas' *Contra Gentiles* on the problem of *duplex veritas*; he will be surprised. And may I further remark that the idea of quoting Gibbon as an authority on this problem is somewhat baroque. The reader will do well also to note the past tense in which the author speaks of Christianity. The realm of Christian experience has practically lost its function in determining the relevant selection of materials; and we shall see that it is not the only realm that has disappeared.

Man, thus, is reduced for the author to the level of an object in the external world; man may be inventive, but he is not the spiritually creative center of society and history; man has lost his singularity and has become a fungible unit. The structure of society is assimilated to that of matter. The science of a social order constituted by persons can produce general rules only with regard to phenomena that are determined by the fungible biological structure of man, or by other structural elements on the periphery of the spiritual core of the person; man has to be reduced to the fungible structures in order to make a science of general rules possible. A system of relevancies of this type will also satisfy the author's pragmatic

desires. Mr. Cairns extends strictures to contemporary legal theorists, as we have seen, because they are occupied with a technology
of law. But he does not condemn technology as such. He only feels
that detached investigation will result in a system of rules that can
be applied more successfully to the solution of social problems,
than the insufficient recipes of scholars who confine their attention too narrowly to the immediate practical problems. A social
science "aims to tell us in advance the perils which attend our various programs; to tell us which is the rational and which the irra-
tional course" (10). The managerial or engineering interest clearly
predominates, assuming blandly that we all know what we want,
that we all want the same, and that the problem of social order does
not lie precisely in the fact that our ideas of order differ in correspondence to our ideas of man.

Mr. Cairns does not overlook the problem entirely. He is aware
that people differ in their opinions about values and that the most
perfect system of technologically usable general rules will not tell
us what to do. His engineering attitude makes him suggest a curious solution to the problem: if we can postulate a science of general rules that does not exist, why not postulate a science of ethical
rules that does not exist? According to the author, we do not have
complete knowledge of legal phenomena unless we possess rules of
evaluation in addition to the rules descriptive of behavior. Such a
science of values "belongs altogether to the future" (144), but that
we shall achieve it in due course the author has no doubt. If only
we take up specific problems one by one, the specific solutions will
"drop of their own accord into a system" (145). The older method,
the medieval, of ordering our problems by referring them to a fundamental attitude of the person toward life and the world as a
whole is broken by the Renaissance (145). Any doubts concerning
the new method of studying specific unrelated problems "were dis-
pelled by the Industrial Revolution and the triumphs of the principle of the Division of Labor" (146). While this argument seems to
have a narcotic effect on Mr. Cairns and makes him see the future
in rosy hues, it has the opposite effect on the reader. For the reader
may remember having heard that an automobile engine is certainly
a triumph of the Division of Labor (capitalized as it befits a divinity), but that the specific parts of the engine do not drop into

place by magic, but because they were made according to the specifications of the designer of the final product. And he may be slightly disturbed by the thought that division of labor without design has sometimes resulted in unpleasantness. If, for instance, we let everybody use his abilities to his best and trust that from the division of labor will emerge somehow a satisfactory order of mankind, we may find to our dismay that the specific parts do not drop at all into their places in a smooth-running order, but that they clash in the ghastly mess of a World War (capitalized to match the divinity of the Division of Labor). I hope I do not have to elaborate the point further in order to make it clear that the spiritual nihilism of Mr. Cairns is pregnant with dangers.

If the nihilism of Mr. Cairns were simply a case of eighteenth-century mechanistic interpretation of man, we would not need to bother about his book. But it is a distinctly modern spiritual nihilism, reflecting the experiences of a philosophic mind. The man of Mr. Cairns is irreligious, he is a-historic and, I have the impression, he may be even a-political in the sense that he has no will to establish a relationship of authority between himself and other men. But he has a very clear ethical consciousness (though Mr. Cairns does not disclose the content of his ethical code) and he reveals an optimistic active desire to improve and stabilize social conditions by "rational" social control. He is socially benevolent, but he is not a benevolent despot; he is a benevolent democrat who dreams of an Huxleyan brave new world minus the differentiation of men into Alphas, Betas, and Gammas.

The intenseness of these sentiments has enabled Mr. Cairns to formulate the central topic of a science of social order; and his formulation stands as that of an important theoretical principle in spite of the curious twist that it receives in the engineering context. We have mentioned earlier the definition of "legal science" as the science of human behavior that reacts against disorder. "The order which exists in human society at any given time is predominantly an achieved order, an invention at the center of which is man; it is not the order of the physical universe, which in physical theory is the product of the blind operation of nature." The social theorist cannot take for granted "an ultimate social order which it is his task to discover. He must assume an ultimate disorder, which through the agency of man's inventiveness and other factors has been changed into order" (54). "Order in social life is wrought from disorder" (53) by means of "creative imagination" (60).

Here at last we tread on classical ground. By the experience of social disorder, human mind is provoked to create order by an act of imagination in accordance with its ordering idea of man. The disorder of the Athenian polis provoked Socrates to stimulate the imagination of his fellow citizens in the direction of true order. He died for his attempt, and Plato created under the impression of this tragedy the great order of the *Republic*, hoping to catch the imagination of the people or at least of a ruler who would impose it on the disordered people. His hope of creating order in Hellas failed, but the *Republic* stands as the first theoretical system of social order in the Western world. Here we can witness the origin of social science in the creative imagination of the philosopher who wishes to overcome disorder. The will to overcome disorder has remained the driving force of the great systems, of the Christian of Saint Augustine and Saint Thomas, and of the later systems originating in the sphere of the national state, until with Giambattista Vico the imaginative creative forces become themselves topical and are so to this day in the great body of science concerned with the theory of social and political myths.

Where does Mr. Cairns stand in relation to his predecessors? With regard to this question the reader will experience a great surprise, for on page 53 he can read that "this approach was first developed" in the year of our Lord 1932 in a paper in the *Political Science Quarterly.*[2]

This is not an occasional remark but the considered opinion of the author. He believes that "at the basis of social thought today is the Holbachian view that man is the work of nature; he exists in nature; he is submitted to her laws; he cannot deliver himself from them. Three centuries of failure should teach us to look in new directions" (52). In the "new direction" we recognize the fact that order is wrought from disorder (53). Christianity is not the only realm of experience that has disappeared; Hellas is out, too, and the theory of the origin of order in the creative myth since Vico is

---

2. Well, Well! This should not cast, however, a reflection on the paper, which is quite good.

swept aside. No reader could be blamed if he parted company with the author and looked "in new directions." But the phenomenon is too overwhelming and too fascinating to be met by such action. There have always been men whose minds had the peculiar bent that we may call, for its most famous instance, the Cartesian. The world had to be wiped out, and only when the *tabula* was *rasa* could they make a new start of theorizing. The grandeur of the *Critique of Pure Reason* is its opening as a monologue spinning a thread of thought out of the mind of the philosopher without regard to anything that has preceded. The style has its merits in philosophy, particularly in the seventeenth and eighteenth centuries, when the thinking Ego emerged as the residue of the wreckage of medieval civilization and the new dimension of history had not yet been fully acquired. But Mr. Cairns is neither a Descartes nor a Kant, but a theorist of "legal science" with an eye on a controlled social order, and we do not live any more in the eighteenth century. The *tabula rasa* attitude is there, but it does not serve to clear a path for speculative action of the *res cogitans*; it rather leaves us face to face with an unknown future, for as we have seen, Mr. Cairns does not replace the past by his own present but projects his idea of science into a distant future.

The implications of this new attitude, which has been in the making since the middle of the nineteenth century, can be made clearer by reflection on a sentence from a speech of Mussolini to his Blackshirts: "The past is behind us, the future is before us, we stand in the present inbetween." Some may consider this sentence an oratorical flourish, but they would be mistaken. Not at all times are the past behind us and the future before us; that happens only when we are in the throes of a violent crisis. Normally the past and the future are present; we do not stand between them, but are moving in the continuous stream of history. The past reaches into our present as the civilizational heritage that has formed us and that we have to absorb into our lives as the precondition for the formation of the future, not in some distant time ahead of us, but in the present of our daily life and work. Mr. Cairns stands on a hilltop, before and behind him stretching a desert of nothingness; the past and the future have shrunk back from his present into solid blocks of "non-existence," the category he uses most frequently. And is there any present left, if past and future have receded? For what is human present but the creative absorption of the past for the purpose of transforming it into the future?

The question is pertinent for the theory of Mr. Cairns. For "in the ordering of human relations, as in other spheres, creative imagination is a necessary factor" (60). The principle is valid, I think, and its elaboration would have given occasion to unfold in form of a system a wealth of materials and interpretations that we possess, ranging from Plato's theory of the origin of order in the mythical forces of the soul to Maurice Hauriou's *idée directrice* as the core of governmental institutions and W. Y. Elliott's theory of personal and institutional myths, et cetera. But again, this whole branch of knowledge comes under the axe; it does not exist. The topic of the creative forces is replaced by a chapter called "The Inventive Process." The choice of vocabulary is characteristic; the term *creative imagination*, which correctly indicates the problem, is used only occasionally, and the main argument is concerned with "invention." "The order which we observe in society is an invention of man" (53). The terminology of invention diverts the problem away from the creative forces of the soul and turns it towards purposive rational action. That "the products of social life, which may be conveniently summed up in the label 'culture,' are inventions" (53) is not a new theory. Critias and Kallikles expounded it at the height of Greek enlightenment when the mythical forces of Athens were dying and the city was ripe for the end. The myth was lost, its problems dissolved into the psychology of the inventive process and the psychology of the motives underlying specific cultural inventions. The heroic attempt of Plato to create a new myth had to fail in this environment.

Mr. Cairns follows the same path. He actually devotes a section to the psychology of the "happy idea" and quotes Helmholtz to the effect that his ideas came most readily " 'during the slow ascent of wooded hills on a sunny day'" (58). Some people get their best ideas when they are drunk, and others attain their most productive mood in even less conventional circumstances. It is a fascinating field— but I wonder whether such stories will help us much in understanding the Declaration of Independence as the basic myth of the order of the American Republic. Mr. Cairns himself does not believe it; and the chapter on invention ends with the inevitable insight that it has not got us anywhere (68). A great opportunity, the opportunity of outlining, at least, the problem of the origin of social order in the creative powers of the person, is wasted.

IV

Mr. Cairns's book abounds in problems on which we have not been able to touch in this review. The reader is particularly referred to the analyses of hypothesis and verification, of change, activity, relation, causality, equilibrium, and the relation between orders. These sections are, however, subordinated to the primary purpose of developing the "model" of the future science. We hope we have brought out the main trend of ideas and attitudes and may now summarize the result.

We started with the "baffling" aspects of the book, with the exhortatory cry for a science of social order that does not exist and with the rejection as non-existent of the body of science that actually does exist. Then we tried to trace these peculiarities to their roots in the metaphysical attitude of the author. We were careful not to deal with his selections and omissions on the level of a critical discussion, which obviously would have been impossible in the face of the author's assigning the status of non-existence to the surrounding world of social science (of which the present writer is an ever-so-humble part). The only occasions for critical remarks were offered, therefore, in the instances in which the author went beyond his verdicts of non-existence and made factually incorrect statements about the subject matter at hand, as in the case of his remarks about the relation of Christian philosophy to the problems of knowledge and truth. For the rest, we preferred to interpret the author's judgments in the light of his system of relevancies. His metaphysical attitude determining the relevancies may be summed up as follows:

The Christian spirituality as well as the historical singularity of the person is annihilated. As no other myth of order is given as an unquestioned enveloping inheritance, man stands on a desert of nothingness without a past; and as the creative center is lost, he carries no order within himself but has to stumble blindly into the future. In the anxiety of his disorder, this man projects his desire for order into the future, hoping that by some miracle the unrelated pieces of the puzzle will fall into place and present him with the order that he himself cannot create. The need for shelter under an order and the inability to create it find their typical expression in seeking refuge in the order of natural science, the only order that is left in our civilization once the spiritual orders are destroyed. The method of natural science will deliver by some black magic the missing order in the form of general rules that can be used in the administration of an ethical program that also will emerge by some magic out of a science of values assembled through the unfailing, planless Division of Labor. And what is that whole order good for, once we have it? Nobody knows. It is an order without meaning, an order at any cost born out of the anxieties of a lost man.

This picture of man and his order is frightening. If the men who by character, intellect, and education should be the pillars of continuity in our civilization, who should be the models of loyalty to our past in order to have a firm grip on the future that is to be shaped by their hands—if these men brush away the past and "march into the future," what shall we expect of the common people? Mr. Cairns's book may not be the ideal scientific treatise, but it certainly is a touching personal document, and it is a terrifying symptom of the disorder in which we live.

Index

Action: science of, 73
Agathon: transcendent being, 77;
  methexis in, 79; Plato's inability to
  define, 79
Aidos, 62
Aletheia, 80
Alexander, 85
Analysis: Voegelin's relentlessness in,
  xv; philosophical questions must
  arise from, 6; analytical legitimacy
  and truth distinguished, 7–8; preanalytical experiences in relation
  to, 9; must precede definition, 11;
  classification of phenomena not
  analysis, 58
Analytical jurisprudence: Voegelin's
  works on, ix; John Austin, law as
  command of sovereign, 109; Cairns's
  denial his theory same as Austin's,
  96
Analytical legitimacy, 7–8
Anthropological civilizations, 76, 77
Aquinas, Thomas: social crisis prompt-
  ing reflections on law, xix, 108;
  rationality of system, 78; *duplex
  veritas* in *Contra Gentiles,* 105
Aristocracy, 60
Aristotle: no philosophy of law, 6; law
  calculated to achieve good order, 26;
  identity of polis after constitutional
  change, 33; status of citizens in polis, 34; polis defined, 41; differing
  analyses of polis, 41; *bios theoretikos,* 41, 57; forms of government,
  42, 60; *spoudaios* as measure of
  order, 63; ethics as science of order
  in soul, 80; natural justice, 81; rec-
  ommendations for action, 82

Articles of confederation, 36
Augustine, 71, 85, 108
Aurelius, Marcus, 71
Austin, John, 46, 56
Authority: normative sources, 68; fu-
  sion of normative authority and
  power, 68
Axis time of mankind, 76

Beatific vision, 78
Bergson, Henri, 76
Bios theoretikos: criterion for civil
  order, 41, 57; relation to happiness,
  74; relation to mature man, 74, 81,
  82; relation to full unfolding of personality, 74, 81, 82
Bodenheimer, Edgar, 91–94
Bodin, Jean: authority of sovereign, 27;
  substance of order according to, 27;
  sources of norms for law, 27, 31

Cairns, Huntington: reply to Voegelin's criticism, xxiv; his *Theory of
  Legal Science* reviewed, 95–112; al-
  leges a legal science does not yet
  exist, 95; critique of Austinian and
  sociological jurisprudence, 96; his
  exaggeration of field of legal science,
  97; orientation toward modern state,
  97; elements of his proposed legal
  science, 97; his assimilation of legal
  science to natural science, 100; failure to recognize philosophical anthropology, 101; his idea of man,
  104, 105, 108, 111; use of Gibbon,
  105; envisions ethics as a natural
  science, 106; unconcern with legal
  technology, 106; his principle of di-

Norms: hypothetical, 31
Nous, 76, 77, 82

Ought: ontological basis, 42–45; arising from tension between true and existential orders, 43; experienced by all humans, 43, 44
Obligation: ontological character of, 42–45
Opening of the soul, 76, 77
Order, primary experiences. *See* Primary experiences of order

Paradoxa (Zenonic): in law envisioned as aggregate of rules, 16–20; in Aristotle's analysis of polis, 33–35
Parsons, Talcott, 98
Participation: as mode of cognition, 79
Pascal, Blaise, 77
Paul, Saint, xx
Peisistratus, 42
Philosophical anthropology: true happiness indicated by, 74; Cairns's failure to recognize, 101; weighing elements of human nature, 103
Philosophical constructions of law: calculation to achieve true order, 26; state-articulated order, 27; law divorced from substantive order, 27–29
Philosophical inquiry: relation to analysis, 6
Philosophies of law: rationality of different kinds, 78
Philosophy: medieval struggle with soul as "form" of man, 35; differentiation from myth, 68; results from opening of soul, 76; original meaning, 76
Philosophy of law: high rationality of Christian, 78; low rationality of positivist, 78
Plato: no philosophy of law, 6; law calculated to achieve true order, 26; forms of government evaluated, 60; cognition of transcendence, 79
Polis: defined, 6; "form" and "nature" in *Politics* III and I, 35; sequences of power structure in, 42
Polity, 60
Positive law theory: varieties of, 72
Positivist legal philosophy, 78
Power: conferring validity to law, 31; condition for true order, 68, 86

Primary experiences of order: listed, 71; return to, 72
Prince: as lawmaker, 27
Projects for law: 48–55; kinds, 49; Plato's and Aristotle's, 51–55; utility of philosophical models, 54, 55
Promulgation of laws, 47–48
Protagoras, 11
Pseudos, 80
Psyche: participation in transcendence, xix, 71, 76, 77; sensorium of transcendence, 76
Punishment, 64
"Pure Theory of Law," 28

Ratio aeterna, 79
Rationality: objective criteria of, 78
Rational science of action: defined, 73
Reason: as condition for true order, 68
Representation of society, 58–59
Representatives in government: issuers of rules to society, 59; source of their authority, 59
Republic, 53, 71, 82, 108
Revelation: condition for true order, 68; differentiation from myth, 68
Revolutions: and law, 35–38
Rickert, Heinrich, 89
Roman Empire: law in, 68
Rousseau, Jean Jacques, 57
Rule and norm: rule as description of pattern, 39; rules dependent on lastingness of social patterns, 39–40; rule as description of "ought," 44; rule as norm, 44–45; rule intends a truth, 44, 45; rule to be heard and obeyed, 45; communication or promulgation of rule, 45–47; public character of legal rule, 45–48; impersonal validity of legal rule, 55–64

Sandoz, Ellis: *The Voegelinian Revolution*, xivn3, xxin4
Science of action, 73
Science of law: requirements for constructing, 87–112 *passim*
Scholastic philosophy, 35
Scott, James Brown, 84–86
Secular national state, 71
Self-understanding, 78
Slaves by nature, 63
Social crises: and reflection on law, 71
"Social instinct" theory, 83
Social order: legal order part of, 30; weight of relation on social side, 30;